THE LITTLE BOOK OF

Life Skills

DEAL WITH DINNER,
MANAGE YOUR EMAIL, MAKE
A GRACEFUL EXIT, AND 152
OTHER EXPERT TRICKS

ERIN ZAMMETT RUDDY

GRAND CENTRAL
PUBLISHING

NEW YORK BOSTON

Grand Central Publishing
Hachette Book Group
1290 Avenue of the Americas, New York, NY 10104
grandcentralpublishing.com
twitter.com/grandcentralpub

First Edition: September 2020

Grand Central Publishing is a division of Hachette Book Group, Inc. The Grand
Central Publishing name and logo is a trademark of Hachette Book Group, Inc.

The publisher is not responsible for websites (or their content)
that are not owned by the publisher.

The Hachette Speakers Bureau provides a wide range of authors for speaking events.
To find out more, go to www.hachettespeakersbureau.com or call (866) 376-6591.

Library of Congress Cataloging-in-Publication Data
Names: Ruddy, Erin Zammett, author.
Title: The little book of life skills : deal with dinner, manage your email, make a
graceful exit, and 152 other expert tricks/Erin Zammett Ruddy.
Description: New York : Grand Central Publishing, 2020.
Identifiers: LCCN 2020014840 | ISBN 9781538751701 (hardcover) |
ISBN 9781538751695 (ebook)
Subjects: LCSH: Self-help techniques. | Life skills.
Classification: LCC BF632 .R83 2020 | DDC 646.7—dc23
LC record available at https://lccn.loc.gov/2020014840

ISBN: 978-1-5387-5170-1 (hardcover), 978-1-5387-5169-5 (ebook)

Printed in the United States of America

LSC-C

10 9 8 7 6 5 4 3 2 1

To my parents, John and Cindy Zammett, for teaching me so many important life skills (but not enough to preclude me from needing to write this book)

Contents

Chapter 3: Work Smarter

Chapter 4: Have a Productive Workday

Chapter 5: Get Organized at Home

Chapter 6: Make Chores Easier

Chapter 7: Clean Anything

Chapter 8: Be Handy

Chapter 9: Dinnertime

Chapter 10: Hosting (and Guesting)

Chapter 11: Self-Care

Chapter 12: Up Your Personal Game

Chapter 13: Up Your Interpersonal Game

Chapter 14: Finish the Day Strong

Introduction

As a writer for major lifestyle magazines for the last twenty years, my job has been to get experts' advice on everything from making a meeting run smoothly to cooking a perfect burger; from asking for a raise to asking for space to asking a neighbor to take down his Christmas lights come March. (All of that is in the book, by the way, except the Christmas lights thing—honestly, you should just move, because that one's really tricky.) I love talking to people who really know their stuff, regardless of what that stuff is (office organization? yes! lawn maintenance? sure! the perfect blowout? 100 percent!). And I know how to deliver that stuff to readers in a way that makes it applicable to their lives, because a highbrow expert isn't always in touch with those of us who don't own cheesecloth or, um, a mop. I can always relate to the reader because I *am* the reader. Yes, even on the stories about, say, decanting your entire pantry into beautifully labeled glass jars. Honestly, am I ever going to do that? Unlikely. Do I want to read about it? Hell, yes!

So, why did I set out to write this particular book? Because I *need* this particular book. My father, a former air traffic controller, has been all about order and mental checklists and a little something he likes to call "doing things the right way the first time" long before it was all trending. When I was growing up, every spring my sisters and I had to help him dry and fold the pool cover once the pool was open for the season. This was a long, methodical ordeal that had eighteen steps and inevitable fire drills ("Quick! Get it off the lawn! It's burning the $★@# grass!"). Then one of us would loudly lament why we couldn't just roll the thing up and call it a day. We'd be answered with a glare. And every fall, as we'd pull the pristine, moldless cover back out of the shed, my father would beam with pride and say something about why we don't half-ass things. The man is efficient, he is organized, and he really does do most things exceptionally well. He also hasn't seen the inside of a control tower since the 1980s but still approaches every task as if the fate of an entire plane of people rests in the balance. Needless to say, things can get intense when he's involved, but, boy, is he a good person to call when you need help making a decision (um, me, every day).

I wish I could say his methods all rubbed off on me and I grew up living my best life surrounded by hospital corners and checked-off to-do lists and keys that never got lost. I did not. I got very little of my father's affinity for precision (and none of my mother's near-professional laundry skills). If I may play psychologist for a moment, I'd say it's because when you have a parent constantly second-guessing the way you're doing seemingly inconsequential things—"Is that how you're going to cut that bagel?" "You can't pack your suitcase that way!" "You really take exit 42 off the expressway, Erin? That red light is a minute and forty-five seconds, I've timed it!"—you sort of give up on striving for "the right way" and settle for "Whatever, I'm still getting it done, aren't I?"

Of course now I'm forty-two and often catch myself midtask (emptying a dishwasher, de-crumbing a counter, arguing with my husband for leaving so many crumbs on the counter) thinking, *Ugh, there must be a better way to do this!* And there is! Keep reading! Like so many of you (just guessing here), I'm craving more efficiency and less stress in my day-to-day routine, a need that's risen steadily as life has gotten more complicated. I mean, there was a time when taking forty-five minutes to zigzag my way through the grocery store like a drunken baby (chomping on a bag of barbecue Baked Lays, obviously) and forgetting two of the seven things I ran in for was a perfectly reasonable way to spend my time. That is no longer the case for a million reasons, but the biggest is probably this: I now have three children, and if you're not staying efficient with kids in your house you will get swallowed whole by a pile of laundry faster than you can say, "If you brushed your teeth, why isn't your toothbrush wet?!" Or so I've been told.

The fact is, there's a particular order in which everything we do in a day *should* be done, a best practice that will heed maximum results with minimal frazzle. There are also important tricks and tips for taking better care of our hearts and minds, things I didn't even know *were* life skills when I went off to college (I also thought fabric softener was detergent, so there's that). But so many of us (hi!) just plow through our busy lives without paying attention to how we're getting from one task to the next. This book is not going to make you feel bad about the way you've been doing things, though. Nor is it going to tell you that what you've been doing your whole life is completely wrong. Because it's probably not. But there's a good chance it's not the most efficient, effective way to do things, either.

But wait, can't you just Google the right way to do...anything? Of course you can. I certainly have. Type in "how to iron a shirt" and you'll get 1.2 million results. (That is not an exaggeration—I just typed it in and that's what came back.) Which is precisely why this book is needed. Who has time to sift through all that often-conflicting content and decide what to trust? Do you really need to watch a seven-minute YouTube tutorial on ironing? And what if— Oh, look! Celebrities without makeup! And now you're in a wormhole of Kim Kardashian's Instagram comments. Hey, it happens to the best of us, but weren't you trying to be more efficient here?! News flash: Looking for advice on the internet can be an overwhelming time suck. And that's not including the fifteen ads you're now going to get for new irons.

So I went straight to the experts. The best of the best in their fields to walk through the basic steps for doing things better. Things that have always tripped me up—keeping a houseplant alive, pumping gas (where I grew up it was illegal to pump your own, so don't make fun), introducing two people over email (why does it always seem awkward?). And the mental and emotional stuff we should all have in our repertoire—talking kindly to ourselves, taking a calming breath, saying hi to someone on a train without having to sit next to them. Every chapter of the book is chock-full of faster, smarter, more streamlined ways to approach the day's to-dos. The reward: more time, less frustration, and the simple pleasure of a job well done. Yes, there is a sense of joy and (OK, Dad) *pride* that comes from doing something right, even if that something is as simple as emptying the dishwasher or storing a pool cover properly. It's not about rushing through the mundane tasks so you can get to your real life (or Netflix queue) faster, it's about slowing down and doing the little things right. Because real life *is* going to the grocery store, and writing emails and sitting at a four-way stop sign wondering who's going to go first.

With the more than 150 how-tos in the book—written in easy, actionable steps we can *all* implement—you'll be able to approach every task with more confidence and carry that calm, can-do attitude throughout your day. You'll accomplish more (and curse less). And you won't have to call your mom every time you spill something on your silk shirt. Who wouldn't want to infuse their day with wins like that? And some of this stuff is downright genius. Not to overstate it, but the day I learned the quick way to tell which side of the car the gas tank is on was a really big day for me (see chapter 2 for that mindblower).

For this book, I've chosen to focus on the basic life skills most of us could use in an average week, because what's the sense in learning how to paint a bathroom or host Thanksgiving if you don't first know the best way to make your bed? These are the tasks that can make the biggest difference with the smallest adjustments, the things that we do over and over and over again but rarely stop to ask, "Wait, am I doing this right?" Perhaps some of the daily chores we realized we could use a refresher on after being stuck at home for months. Just me?

I've organized the chapters in the order in which you might need these abilities on any given day. From getting up, getting ready, and getting out the door with minimum hassle, to having a productive, satisfying workday and figuring out what the heck to order for lunch, to advice on getting through all your housework and yard-work pain free, preparing dinner (ugh, again?!), and getting a good night's sleep. There are also chapters focused on being your best self in your head and your heart, as well as in your relationships with others (yes, how to argue productively *is* a life skill).

Oh, and you know how a food blogger lures you to click with the promise of the greatest lemon tart recipe *ever* and then there's a 1,200-word essay about her great-aunt's lemon farm and the limoncello she drank during her gap year in Tuscany and you're, like, but where's the $%★@ recipe? *The Little Book of Life Skills* jumps to the recipe for all of it. No backstories or lengthy explanations, no need to skim until the juicy parts. Just the thing, the order in which to do the thing, and the many fist pumps that will inevitably follow when you master that thing.

The book can be read cover to cover, or you can look in the table of contents for whatever you need help with right this minute. You can even zigzag your way through if you like. I promise not to judge the way you read a book about the right way to do things—as long as you promise not to tell my dad I still totally take exit 42. Every. Damn. Time.

THE LITTLE BOOK OF

Life Skills

WAKE UP AND GET READY FOR THE DAY

GET OUT OF BED

1. DO NOT hit the snooze button. RESIST.
2. Open your eyes (a "1-2-3 go!" can help if you're stuck on this step).
3. Swing your legs over the side of the bed and plant your feet on the floor.
4. Take 5 deep breaths.
5. Drink a full glass of water.
6. Get outside into the sunlight if you can (or hang out near a window—crack it for the unfiltered rays). Aim for 15 minutes, ideally.

THE EXPERT:

Michael J. Breus, Ph.D., aka "the Sleep Doctor," is a renowned sleep expert and author of *The Power of When*.

THE EXPLANATION:

Starting your day with a snooze is the worst thing you can do; your body cannot get back into a deep sleep in those seven to nine minutes, so you're just giving yourself light ZZZs that can ultimately make you more groggy. Instead, before you even stand up, take those deep breaths to get oxygen to your body and brain so both can function at their best. You lose almost a liter of water each night through the humidity in your breath (kinda cool, kinda gross), so drinking a full glass will replenish and hydrate. Then sunlight—ideally ten to fifteen minutes—which turns off the "melatonin faucet" in your brain and lifts that groggy morning fog. Get outside (without sunglasses) within fifteen minutes of waking for the best results. If the sun isn't up when you are (or you live in, say, the Pacific Northwest) turn on the lights. Blue light—which is in sunlight, LED bulbs, our electronic devices and fluorescents—is what you need most in the a.m. Or consider a light therapy box, a device you can sit or work next to which gives off bright light that mimics sunlight.

Bonus

Want to feel even more bright-eyed? If you're taking a morning shower, slowly decrease the temperature at the end. You don't have to make it ice-cold, but it should give you a mild chill, which will force all the blood to your trunk, and is very alerting. Cool!

START EVERY DAY WITH A POSITIVE ATTITUDE

1. As soon as you wake up, write down 3 things you're grateful for (be specific and don't just say "the sunny day" though you can totally be grateful for that). Keep a journal by your bedside to make this step easier.
2. Write down something great that happened in the last 24 hours—this can be a big thing or a small thing but, again, be specific.
3. Exercise (aim for 30 minutes if you can). FOR TIPS ON GETTING YOURSELF TO WORK OUT AND GETTING THE MOST OUT OF IT SEE PAGE 192.

4. Pray or meditate. FOR EASY MEDITATION HOW-TOS SEE PAGES 178 AND 180.

5. Do one random act of kindness for someone.

THE EXPERT:

Hoda Kotb is the coanchor of *Today* and author of several best-selling books including *I Really Needed This Today*, which features 365 sayings to inspire and uplift. One reason Hoda always seems so genuinely happy? She writes ("scribbles") in her journal every single morning to remind herself how lucky she is.

THE EXPLANATION:

When you wake up in the morning and the first thing you do is write down three good things and one great thing, it starts to change the way you think—instead of waking up going "Oh God…" and thinking about something that upset you the night before or what you have to do later, your brain starts changing. It helps you reframe your whole day to be a *good* day. Specifics help, so don't just be grateful for the sunrise or being alive (though Hoda is grateful for all of those things). Instead, think of something small and specific—like the guy who held the door for you last night even though he had three bags in his hand and could have let it swing shut. This helps you stay aware of the thousands of reminders of goodness around you. You actually start to look for them! And exercise because, well, endorphins. It doesn't have to always be super strenuous, even a walk around the block counts. And one of the best ways to get out of any funk is to do something nice for somebody else. This can be as simple as buying a coworker a cup of coffee when you run out to get yours.

Bonus

Hoda's other positivity hack: Good music. Create a playlist you love and use as needed.

MAKE YOUR BED

"You spend a third of your life in bed, it should be a place that feels good and gives you comfort. And it only takes two minutes to make it look great!"

—Ariel Kaye

1. Pull back all the covers and start at the foot of the bed to assess the situation—every morning is a little different in terms of what things look like.

2. Make sure your fitted sheet is pulled down all the way and securely tucked in at the foot and then around the whole bed so it's taut and you have a nice clean surface (move your pillows to a bench or side table, or just work around them).

3. If you sleep with a top sheet, pull it up, giving it a good shake as you go (think about that parachute you used to play with in gym class and mimic that movement). Next, smooth it out with your hand and tuck it in to your liking. You can opt for taut hospital corners or go for a more relaxed, lived-in look. Another option is to forgo the top sheet altogether. (A top sheet often ends up tangled at the foot of the bed and can feel like an unnecessary extra layer.)

4. Give the duvet or comforter the same big parachute shake and make sure the duvet insert is properly aligned in all four corners, then spread it out evenly across the bed.

5. If you have a lot of pillows, pull the top sheet and duvet cover entirely up to the top of the bed and smooth out. If you don't do a lot of pillows, you can fold the top sheet and duvet back a third of the way down the bed for a layered look.

6. Plump your pillows to get them full looking, then arrange with the shams against the headboard and the pillows in front, or vice versa (if you've pulled down your covers, you want the

pillows to stay on top of the exposed bottom sheet). Add any decorative pillows.

7. If you have a quilt, fold it in thirds and lay it out across the foot of the bed with the open side facing the bottom, smoothing out any creases with your hands.

THE EXPERT:

Ariel Kaye is the founder and CEO of Parachute, a modern lifestyle brand, and author of *How to Make a House a Home: Creating a Purposeful, Personal Space*. She first launched Parachute as an online-only brand with a curated assortment of bedding products (it was named after the way the fabric billows when you shake out your sheets!). Parachute has since opened brick-and-mortar stores across the country and expanded to include bath, furniture, tabletop, and a baby collection.

THE EXPLANATION:

Deal with the foot of the bed first because, well, nothing is more frustrating than when things come undone in the middle of the night. (Did you sleep like a corpse or a tornado? The damage will be different each day.) When you're pulling up the covers, getting that big parachute lift is helpful to shake out wrinkles, freshen the linens, and make sure everything gets evenly distributed. If you're a more-the-merrier pillow person (Ariel is), you don't also need to fold things down—you want the bed to have a layered, textured look but not be too busy.

Everyone's bed-making method will be slightly different and that's fine, so long as you do it every damn day. Yes, you have the time (it takes two or three minutes). Research shows that a made bed actually boosts happiness. It makes the room feel instantly organized and makes *you* feel organized, too—nothing better than checking something off the to-do list before you've even had your coffee. Oh, and if you ever wanted a reason to *not* use a top sheet (Europeans don't and many companies, including Parachute, now sell sheets separately for this reason), it will save you about sixty seconds when making your bed. Boom!

Bonus

Ariel's thoughts on thread count: It's a marketing gimmick that doesn't have much to do with actual quality. (Anything over 400 is a result of fiber manipulation, which means synthetics were likely used to make it feel softer.) What really matters: caliber of the fiber, staying away from chemicals and synthetics, and the way the fabric is woven. So what *should* you buy? If you tend to sleep hot at night, you might want percale sheets, as its one-thread-over-one-under weave gives the fabric ultra breathability. If you tend to be cool at night, sateen is lustrous with a soft feel from its four-over-one-under weave, which also keeps you warmer. Avoid anything that says "wrinkle resistant"—that's often coated in formaldehyde. Really, any claim that makes you think, *How would they do that?!* means it's generally done with something toxic that you wouldn't want against your skin. Instead look for sheets that say OEKO-TEX certified, which means there are no toxic chemicals, artificial dyes, or synthetic finishes used from beginning to end.

FOR ARIEL'S TIPS ON FOLDING A FITTED SHEET AND PUTTING ON A DUVET COVER WITHOUT LOSING IT, SEE PAGES 97 AND 100.

GIVE YOURSELF THE PERFECT BLOWOUT

1. Spray hair with a heat protectant hair spray to shield it from the high temps, and loosely blow-dry to 70–80 percent dry (or let it air-dry to this point).

Step 1

2. If you have bangs, dry them first so you can set them properly. If you're looking for a specific part, create that first, too.

3. Section the top layers of your hair and secure with a clip. (You'll start drying the bottom layer and work your way up and out.)

Step 2

4. Put a concentrating nozzle on your hair dryer—as long as you use a heat protectant, you can safely use the high setting.

5. Take 2-inch sections of hair into a round brush and overdirect the root (*overdirecting* means to blow-dry in the opposite direction, toward your scalp, to set the root).

Step 3

6. Place the brush under the section, and lift the brush up with tension for volume. Place the dryer on top, and follow the hair and the brush down, holding the nozzle parallel (about a half-inch away) to the section to help close the cuticle.

Step 4

7. Roll the ends under. Hold for 3–4 seconds, and then remove the brush downward.

8. Repeat with all sections, removing clips as you go. Finish by blowing down over all the hair with a cool shot on the hair dryer. Tame any stubborn pieces—like that frizz by your ear—with a flat iron on low heat. Don't touch your hair until it's fully cooled because you want your hair to maintain the set.

Step 5   Step 6

THE EXPERT:

Sarah Potempa is a celebrity stylist (her clients include Lea Michele, Emily Blunt, Camila Cabello, and Reese Witherspoon) and the inventor of the patented Beachwaver® curling iron. She's the CEO of Beachwaver Co.®, which provides innovative hair tools and products to customers worldwide. She's styled hair on photo shoots for *Vogue*, *Marie Claire*, *Vanity Fair*, and *W* magazine and appeared on *Today*, *The Real*, and *Extra!*

THE EXPLANATION:

Ideally you want your hair to be about 70–80 percent dry by the time you take your blow-dryer to it, so use that break to do your makeup, get dressed, maybe even meditate. Resist the urge to just throw your head down and dry it that way; it will fray the cuticle too much. And avoid roughing or twisting your hair up with a regular towel, especially if you have curly hair or are prone to frizz (in lieu of rough towels, you can use T-shirt material to absorb moisture without damaging hair). Sectioning saves time, so use a strong-hold sectioning clip to pin back hair layer by layer as you go. A gentle targeted air flow will close the cuticle and polish the hair. (Imagine the hair cuticles as roof shingles—the shingles point down, so if you direct the dryer at your hair perpendicularly, you're fraying it by opening those shingles again.) As soon as a blowout is done, a lot of people immediately start touching their hair. Yes, it feels good, but you don't want to mess with all the work you just did. In order for the physical change to set in, you need the hair to completely cool down before handling it.

A word about washing your hair:

A great blowout starts in the shower. Shampoo should be focused on your scalp so you're cleansing it of natural oils and product buildup that could be weighing down your roots. Conditioner is really what's meant for your *hair*, where you put in moisture and give it the correct ingredients to have a good hair day. Apply conditioner only to the middle and ends of your hair. (If you put conditioner on or near your roots, it will weigh your hair down.) The ends, which have been around the longest, are the least healthy and need the most moisture. Rinse with cool water to close the cuticles.

A word about sulfate-free shampoo:

Sodium lauryl sulfate is an emulsifier and foaming agent used in a ton of common cosmetic products and industrial cleaners. It's the main ingredient in a lot of shampoo brands, but it's a really intense cleanser and irritant—think of it like dish soap. So if you're not shampooing properly (i.e., you're washing the ends of your hair instead of your scalp), you're basically using dish soap on your hair and fraying the cuticle—and setting yourself up for a bad hair day every day.

Bonus

Sarah's tips for extending the life of your blowout:

- Use dry shampoo *at your roots.* A lot of people use dry shampoo only on the very top layer of their hair, but then that hair falls back on greasy, flat pieces by your ears and your neck. To create a solid foundation, lift the hair starting at your ear level, and spray underneath each layer. Repeat in 1-inch sections up to the top layer. You want the shampoo to absorb oil from the root.
- Tame flyaways by spraying your brush with hair spray and brushing that through your hair to distribute evenly. In a pinch you can roll the hair spray can (it's always cold!) to lock down flyaways. (Sarah does this on photo shoots all the time.)
- At night pull your hair into two high, loose buns. Take the hair on the left side of your part and roll it away from your face into a bun, then take the hair on the right side of your part and roll it

away into a bun (you'll look like Princess Leia). Secure them with soft scrunchies or large hairpins. One topknot in a scrunchie can also work if your hair will hold that, though it can cause hair to kink because one side is fighting to go the other way. Two buns prevents that.

- Put your hair into a loose, low braid to sleep in. This is particularly successful if you have long hair and like some movement to your blowout. When you remove the braid, the cuticle is still smooth and flat but the hair has a soft, pretty wave to it.

- Avoid regular elastics; they'll put a kink in your hair. Scrunchies, hairpins, and silk headbands are the way to go. (Silk pillowcases are also great because the material won't fray your hair cuticles while you sleep.)

WASH AND MOISTURIZE YOUR FACE

"The best foundation is healthy skin."

—Nyakio Grieco

1. Cleanse and pat your face dry.
2. Put a few drops of face oil into your hands and rub them together to warm it up. Pat it into your face, starting at your neck and working your way up to cheeks, nose, and forehead, then back to your chin.
3. If you have dry skin and want to layer another moisturizer on top, do that now. Pat it into your skin following the same bottom-up path you did with the oil.
4. Put on your eye cream by dotting it onto the fingertip of your ring finger. Starting on the inside working out, place four dots of the cream under your eye. Use that same finger to dot back and forth over and over until the cream dissolves (you're almost

giving yourself a little lymphatic massage here). Repeat under the other eye.

5. Once your moisturizers are soaked in and dry, apply your sunscreen.[1] FOR MORE ON SUNSCREEN SEE PAGE 12. (Every single person should be wearing sunscreen every single day no matter how dark your skin is.) If you use a hydrating sunscreen, you can skip the moisturizer step.

THE EXPERT:

Nyakio (Neh-Kay-Oh) Grieco is a skin-care expert and the founder of Nyakio beauty, a cruelty-free, clean, and green skin-care line. Nyakio's grandfather was a medicine man in Kenya, so she incorporates the use of oils—and other African ingredients—into her brand.

THE EXPLANATION:

Everybody should be washing their face, even when you're not wearing makeup, even when you don't feel like your skin is dirty (our pores still take in a lot of crud from the environment throughout the day). Using *oil* on your *face*? Yes! Our skin is made up of oil, and as we age we lose those oils. People say, "Oh, but I have oily skin, I'm prone to breakouts." Then you probably need oil even more than someone with dry skin because your skin is working too hard to produce its own oil to compensate—which causes irritation and breakouts. In order to keep skin balanced and in tip-top shape, we need to *use* oil to *fight* oil. Whenever you're applying product to your neck or face, always start at the lowest point and move up—never pull your skin down (gravity is doing enough of that). And pat the product on. Especially with the very sensitive skin under our eyes. You don't

---

1. At night, skip the sunscreen and use a heavier moisturizer—that's when your skin is in repair mode. Bonus points if you add a sleep mask (look for one with chamomile or rose hip, so it doubles as an aromatherapy treatment—breathing in those scents helps you relax).

want to stretch and pull it by smearing the product back and forth. Tapping also helps massage the puff away and wakes you up in the morning! A good hydrating sunscreen is worth it for *everyone* (there are more cases of skin cancer in people of color than ever before). Put it next to your toothpaste—*that's* how regular it should be.

A word about high-quality natural skin-care products:

Use them. Just like our body doesn't know how to digest, say, margarine, our skin doesn't know how to absorb synthetic products that are packed with a ton of preservatives. You want your skin to drink up the product; you don't want it to sit on top of your skin. When trying a new skin-care product, no matter how natural, Nyakio says to patch-test it first. The bottom of the jawline is a great place because if it makes you break out, it won't be right smack in the middle of your forehead.

Pro tip: Exfoliate two times a week to slough off dull, dry skin cells. Our pores are being taxed by the environment, sweat, and stress—when we slough off those dry, hardened skin cells it helps the glowy skin come to the surface. It's important to remember that even though we can't see our pores, they're getting dirty like the rest of our body.

APPLY SUNSCREEN

"There's only one skin-care product that helps mitigate the visual signs of aging from the sun, and that's sunscreen."

—Chris Birchby

1. Apply 30 minutes before going out into the sun if you're using classic sunscreen (if you're using a mineral active sunscreen, you can apply right before going out).

2. Start with your face (invest in a special facial sunscreen and put it on *over* any moisturizer).
3. Remember your ears!
4. Work your way down your body, covering every bit of skin that will be exposed (you'll use about 1 ounce of sunscreen for the full body and about a quarter teaspoon for your face).
5. If you're going outside with your feet uncovered, don't forget the tops of your feet.
6. Reapply every two hours or after vigorous physical activity or going in the water (use extra caution near water, snow, and sand as they reflect the damaging rays of the sun, boosting your chances of a burn).
7. Do this every damn day, winter or summer, clouds or sunshine.

THE EXPERT:

Chris Birchby is the founder and CEO of COOLA, an organic sunscreen line sold around the world. After both his parents had melanoma diagnoses (and fortunate recoveries), Chris started looking at his own bad sun habits and re-realized the importance of frequent sunscreen use. Unable to find any wearable, healthy sunscreens, he decided to create his own.

THE EXPLANATION:

The sun's rays are the strongest from 10 a.m. to 2 p.m., but up to 20 percent of harmful rays can penetrate your skin even on a cloudy day. And 90 percent of the visible signs of aging are due to sun damage. Facial skin is the most sensitive and susceptible to sun and pollution damage, so start there—it's critical to find a noncomedogenic formula (that won't clog pores) specifically formulated for the face. Look for a lightweight, hydrating sunscreen to replace your morning moisturizer (that said, when you feel the need for extra hydration, apply moisturizer *underneath* your sunscreen). Pay attention when you're applying so you don't miss a spot—ears and tops of feet are two of the most forgotten areas (and sunburned feet can be a real bummer on your beach vacation). The trick for both kids and adults: Find sunscreen that feels and looks good on (no thick white caking) so that applying it isn't such a chore.

A word about SPF:

SPF stands for "sun protection factor." Sunscreens are classified by an SPF number, which refers to their ability to deflect UVB rays. The SPF rating is calculated by comparing the amount of time needed to burn sunscreen-protected skin versus unprotected skin. You want to find a broad spectrum SPF 30 or higher to protect not only against sunburn, but reduce the risk of skin cancer and premature skin aging caused by the sun.

Pro tip: Wear sunscreen even when you're inside. Windows do not block UVA rays (UVA rays won't make you burn but they can definitely cause damage). And research shows that blue light (also known as high-energy visible light, or HEV) that emits from the screens on cell phones, computers, tablets, and TVs, as well as from fluorescent and LED lighting, can reach deeper into our skin than UVA and UVB rays. Yet another reason to unplug!

PUT ON YOUR MAKEUP

1. Apply primer if you're using it (you should try; it locks in your moisturizer and keeps makeup on longer).
2. Put on foundation, *then* concealer.
3. Brush on your blush (followed by highlighter if that's in your repertoire—and it should be, girl!). SEE PAGE 16 FOR HIGHLIGHTER HOW-TO.
4. Build your eye shadow by covering the lid with a light shade, and then using a deeper shade in the crease.

5. Apply eyeliner.
6. Put on mascara. Do not be shy here—make sure you get it all the way to the base of the lash.
7. Do your eyebrows. SEE PAGE 18 FOR EVERYTHING ON BROWS.
8. Finish the look with lipstick or gloss.

THE EXPERT:

Mally Roncal is a celebrity makeup artist and the founder of the cosmetics line Mally Beauty (she's been on QVC for fifteen years!). Her past clients include Jennifer Lopez, Beyoncé, and Heidi Klum. Mally is featured regularly on *Rachael Ray*, *The Wendy Williams Show*, and *Good Morning America* as the TV makeover queen and is the author of *Love, Lashes, and Lipstick: My Secrets for a Gorgeous, Happy Life*.

THE EXPLANATION:

Experts used to advise you apply eye makeup first, because "fallout" from your shadow would get all over your just-done face. But products have evolved so much that fallout is not really an issue anymore (if your eye shadow is kicking up that much dust, it's time for a new one). Plus, starting with your "complexion work" gives you a smooth foundation (literally and figuratively), so you're not distracted by dark circles or blemishes when doing your eyes. Applying blush before eye makeup is key because color on your cheeks may mean you need less color around the eyes. The purpose of eye shadow is to lift and open up the eye, and then eyeliner defines the lash line and makes the lashes look thicker (you put it on after the shadow so you can see it). Just keep the line thin—the fatter it is, the smaller your eye will seem because it makes the eye appear to recede back into the head, and you could wind up looking like two holes in a bedsheet. Brows come next to last, as they'll have their own personality based on what you do with your eyes (i.e., bolder eyes need a bolder brow).

Pro tip: If you're going for a bold lip color, you need to make sure your mouth is prepared—exfoliate, wax, pluck—because a dark color draws everyone's eye directly to your lip. Choose a lipstick that has a semi matte, not a wet or greasy formula. For more control use the opposite side of the bullet of the lipstick (just flip it and use the pointy side). Then do your liner, or take a small eyeliner or lip brush, swipe it in the lipstick, and use that to clean up the line around the mouth. To further sharpen the edges, and for a nice finishing touch, take a little bit of concealer on your concealer brush and go around the corners of the mouth. Mwah!

PUT ON HIGHLIGHTER

"What's beautiful about highlighter is that it lights up what you love. Everyone can use it and should—not only to finish a look but on its own for a one-product glow."

—Lisa Sequino

1. Do your highlighter *after* you've put on the rest of your makeup—or in *lieu* of the rest of your makeup.
2. Apply it to the area around the outsides of your eyes, creating a C shape starting from your brow bone, going over to your temple, and back in to your cheekbone. Blend well.
3. Tap it on to the high points of your face—cheekbones, brow bones, bridge of your nose, tip of your chin—then blend. (To find those high points, look out a window or at a source of light with your mirror in your hand—where the light hits naturally are your high points.)
4. Swipe the highlighter right above your lip to make it look a little fuller.

5. Double-check that wherever you've put the highlighter, you've blended well—it should look natural, rather than like a stripe.
6. Avoid putting it on the sides of your nose or directly underneath your eye.

THE EXPERT:

Lisa Sequino is the global general manager and senior vice president of BECCA Cosmetics, a cruelty-free brand with a mission to create effortlessly glowing complexion products for every skin type and color (they're known for their creamy highlighters, which melt right into your skin). Lisa is responsible for building BECCA's global brand equity and developing the brand strategy (she also wore nothing but highlighter on her face for three months after having her baby and managed to feel normal).

THE EXPLANATION:

Highlighter is all about proper application, so whether you're putting it on a bare face with just moisturizer or using it to finish a full face of makeup, the key is to put it on the *right places*. It should draw attention to the eyes, to the lips, and to the overall vitality of your face (the reason the high points are so important is that it adds dimension). The purpose of a highlighter is to amplify what we already have (as they say at BECCA, it should illuminate us inside and out). Everyone has that one picture of themselves that they wish they could go back to, their "I look amazing" shot, and it's usually at the beach or after a beach vacation where you're feeling that glow. Highlighter does the same thing—it gives you the appearance of being in great lighting all day long. So when you look at a picture of yourself with the right application of highlighter, you're going to see that natural, beautiful, amazing glow you had when you were maybe eighteen... or in Miami. Yes, please!

Bonus

No highlighter on you? No problem. In a pinch, just put clear lip gloss on your cheekbones—the reflectivity will give you a glossy, wet look, which is really cool especially at night. If you want something driving more vitality and radiance into your skin, take a red or pink lipstick and rub it on your fingers, then blend it into your cheekbones. You can even brush on a shimmery, skin-toned eye shadow for a little glow and radiance.

Pro tip: Highlighter can also be used to light up your cleavage, shoulders, and legs. You'll look polished, sun-kissed, and glowy— yes, yes, and yes!

DO YOUR BROWS

"It used to be all you need is mascara and you're ready to leave the house; now all you need are good brows!"

—Jimena Garcia

1. Use a primer—a little castor oil applied with a spoolie brush works wonders. It's light, not stiff, and will help condition the hair. (A spoolie is the little wand thing like what comes in a mascara tube—you can buy them separately at the drugstore or online.)
2. Brush your brows up to see what you're working with.
3. Use a brow pencil that matches your natural brow color (the pencil goes on the skin to fill in any sparse areas). Make short, soft, dash-like strokes that mimic your natural brow hair.
4. Apply brow powder in a slightly lighter color (combining different shades will add texture). Use an angled brush to help define the shape of your brows.

5. Set the hair with a brow gel (brush up near the inside if you want that full, natural brow look).
6. Don't overdo it—you want to be sure you can see *hair*, not just makeup. Remember to leave texture on your face.

THE EXPERT:

Jimena Garcia is a highly sought-after celebrity brow artist who's been shaping brows all over the world for more than twenty years. She was recently appointed Chanel's first-ever brow artist.

THE EXPLANATION:

Brows are usually the finishing touch—the last thing you do when doing your makeup. But they may be all you need. Start with the pencil for your detail-oriented work—create a shape or fill in a hole. The powder is more of a shadow for the brow, and it doesn't compete with the texture of the hair. Combing through a colored brow gel will hold the hairs in place. **Brow hack:** If you don't have a tinted brow gel you can use your brown eye shadow and an essential oil—apply using a little spoolie or even a toothbrush. Brown mascara will also do the trick in a pinch—just whoosh it up like you would a gel. Or keep an aloe leaf in the refrigerator, cut it, brush through the meat of the plant with a spoolie, and use that as brow gel. It's super cool and totally works!

A word about brow tint:

Tinting is a great way to bring your brow to its fullest state—the dye picks up all of the baby hairs and coats every hair, creating an even tone and shine. Natural hair has a tendency to be ashy and flat. Even if you have black hair, tinting makes it shinier and richer (you can also lighten your brows if you have very strong features and are looking to soften).

A word about grooming:

Use a tweezer to take off the excess fuzz/hair not in your brow or hair that's away from the general shape you're going for—but don't pluck every day. And don't pluck hairs in areas you want growth—trim them with little scissors instead so you leave a short hair, which maintains the fullness of the brow (otherwise you create a hole). If you have a rogue hair that's growing in the wrong direction, tweeze it out by pulling it in the direction you *want* it to grow. (The bulb of the hair within the layer of the skin can be redirected so that hair can be taught to grow the right way—amazing, right?!)

A word about growing out your brows:

You want your brows to be growing on the same cycle, which may mean letting them grow out so that the stages aren't uneven (which causes you to pluck all the time, which you don't want). Try mixing castor oil, vitamin E, and sweet almond oil (the same amount of each) into a small jar and apply the mixture before bed. And you know the old grandma tale that if you brush your hair a hundred strokes every night, your hair will grow? Try it with your brows, it helps!

BLEND THE PERFECT SMOOTHIE

"Drinking a smoothie in the morning is like meditation. It helps you set your intention for the day."

—Catherine McCord

1. Buy frozen fruit—it's often cheaper and can even taste better than fresh depending on the season. Store the bags together in a plastic bin in the freezer so you always know what you have and don't have to stand there with the door open searching.

2. Always keep some bananas in the freezer—a half a banana will make your smoothie really creamy and has a ton of potassium.

3. Pick a few superboosters to have on hand—these are supplements you can add to your smoothie to amplify its nutritional impact (hemp seeds, chia seeds, bee pollen, protein powder).

4. Choose your liquid to go with your ingredients; anything from cow's milk to pea milk (it's really good!) to coffee or just plain water (coconut water works really well with greens). For a low- or no-calorie liquid, green tea is great. And it will give you energy without the same caffeine kick as coffee!

5. Wash fresh produce right before putting it into your smoothie, not ahead of time. (Bonus: You don't have to dry it!) FOR MORE ON WASHING PRODUCE SEE PAGE 127.

6. When assembling your smoothie, put softer or fresher fruits in first, like bananas or avocado, then frozen items and greens—aim for a mix of 2–3 vegetables and 2–3 fruits.

7. Add any powders or seeds on top.

8. Pour your liquid in last (generally about ¾ to 1 cup per serving) and blend it up, baby!

THE EXPERT:

Catherine McCord is a food expert and founder of the Weelicious brand, a trusted content resource (and gorgeous Instagram) focused on family and food. She's the author of *Smoothie Project*, *Weelicious*, and *Weelicious Lunches*. (She and her family start every single day with a smoothie.)

THE EXPLANATION:

The smoothie you make will depend on what you have on hand. You can really mix and match to your own tastes—some people like tropical, some like chocolate peanut butter (does anyone not?!), some like hard-core green detox. It can also depend on the day.

Regardless, frozen is your friend. For fruit and vegetables, you can buy organic cheaper when it's frozen, you can have strawberries in the dead of winter, and you never have to wash or cut anything. Good greens to have on hand: spinach, kale, chard. But greens are just the tip of the iceberg; there are so many other vegetables you can get in a smoothie that you won't even taste. Even broccoli. **Catherine's favorite hack:** frozen cauliflower. A cup has about two grams of protein, twenty calories, and it makes your smoothies really creamy without changing the color or the taste. The goal for a smoothie is to get as much bang for your buck as you can. Just remember to put in your powders and seeds and nuts at the end, right before the liquid. If you put them in the bottom, they can get stuck.

Bonus

Make-ahead smoothies: If you're time-challenged in the a.m. make a big batch of smoothies on a Sunday; divide it among seven mason jars, filling them three-quarters full (so they can expand and not crack the glass), seal tightly, and freeze. Each night, transfer one to the fridge, and in the morning just shake it up and go. (You can store a smoothie in the freezer for up to three months.) This is also a good trick if you're up before the rest of your house and don't want to wake them all up with the whirring of the blender. If you're saving your smoothie to drink later at work, add a squeeze of lemon to keep the color bright.

What superbooster is right for you? You do not need to add any, but if you're looking to get the most bang for your buck, why not?

- Is your energy low? Try spirulina or matcha powder or blue algae (it's from the sea and has tons of micronutrients).
- Need more fiber in your life? Chia seeds!
- If you're working on your hair, skin, and nails, add collagen. (According to Catherine, every woman over the age of 35 should take collagen peptides for their joints, skin, hair, and nails—on it!).

• For an immunity booster, try bee pollen. It's also high in protein, and if you buy *local* bee pollen, it can help with seasonal allergies. (Bee pollen is Catherine's secret weapon—her entire family has it in their smoothies every day.)

Greens hack: Next time you have a bunch of greens on hand, whip up a quick batch of "green cubes"—blend two cups of greens, one banana, and a cup of your choice of milk, water, or coconut water, and pour into ice cube trays and freeze overnight. Transfer the cubes to a freezer bag or container and store in the freezer for up to four months. Add two cubes to your smoothies! (The banana adds a touch of sweetness, but you can leave it out if you're a greens purist.)

COOK CREAMY, NEVER-OVERCOOKED SCRAMBLED EGGS

"Eggs are unpretentious but challenging; they are the perfect medium for the cook to blend proper technique with taste."
—Jacques Pépin

1. Break six large eggs into a bowl and add salt and pepper (about ½ teaspoon salt and ¼ teaspoon freshly ground black pepper).
2. Beat the eggs with a fork or whisk to mix well (poke the yokes first with the fork for easy mixing).
3. Set ¼ cup of the raw eggs aside.
4. Melt about 2 tablespoons of unsalted butter in a heavy saucepan over medium heat.
5. When the butter is foaming, pour in the remaining eggs and cook, stirring gently with the whisk.

6. Keep cooking and whisking pretty much continuously until the mixture gets very creamy. The eggs should have the smallest possible curds.

7. Continue cooking, moving the pan in and out of the heat as necessary, until you can see the bottom of the pan as the whisk is drawn through the eggs.

8. Remove the pan from the heat; the eggs will continue cooking, especially around the edges of the pan—that's OK.

9. Add the reserved raw eggs and, if you fancy, two tablespoons of sour cream or heavy cream, and keep mixing until everything is incorporated.

10. Transfer to a serving dish so the eggs stop cooking, and serve as soon as possible.

THE EXPERT:

Jacques Pépin is a world-renowned chef, author, television host (he used to do a cooking show with Julia Child!), and dean of special programs at the International Culinary Center. He's a founder of the American Institute of Wine and Food and sits on the board of trustees of the James Beard Foundation.

THE EXPLANATION:

Is this the healthiest way to prepare eggs? No. Does that matter? Also no. It's Jacques Pépin, people! He judges chefs on their ability to make a proper French omelet; this man knows his oeufs. (And if you cut the butter and cream and simply follow the cooking technique, it still produces perfect eggs every time.) The eggs are stirred almost continuously to allow only the smallest possible curds to form which produces the creamiest possible mixture. The eggs will have a tendency to set and harden around the bottom edge of the pan, so make sure you're getting your whisk out there, too. Stirring in some of the reserved uncooked eggs at the end prevents the eggs from overcooking after they've reached the proper consistency (the pan and already-cooked eggs will still generate enough heat to cook the raw eggs). The measurements above should feed three people (or two very hungry people!). You can scale up or down depending on how many people you're cooking for. Mastering eggs of any kind takes practice, but once you have basic techniques in your back pocket you'll always be able to whip something up. (Jacques is even a fan of eggs for dinner; add anything from ham and cheese to truffle sauce and caviar!)

STAY CURRENT ON THE NEWS (QUICKLY AND WITHOUT SPIRALING)

"Opinion journalism is an excuse for a lack of discipline. Seek out journalists who prioritize you and the facts over partisanship."

—Jenna Lee

1. Acknowledge the importance of staying informed (it's important) and commit to it.
2. Know that it's not all or nothing—just because you don't have two hours to curl up with a newspaper and an oat milk latte doesn't mean you can't stay current. Even a few minutes a day will add up to your being an informed person.
3. Curate a few trusted sources *across different outlets* and create your *own* "news family," so to speak. Stick with them, rather than surfing around for news.
4. Find a journalist you trust and keep up with what they're writing (if you're looking for nonpartisan information, find someone with a true journalism background).
5. If you want an opinion, seek out an editorialist with a body of work that's consistent and thought provoking.

6. Sign up for the daily email briefing sent out each morning from your favorite news source (major news outlets will generally cover the same stories, so pick one and stick with it to avoid inundation); or listen to a daily radio briefing or podcast.

7. Keep up to date on three main topics: how the economy is doing, where our soldiers are (and why), and one piece of cutting-edge technology or a recent health innovation (this is a great way to add optimism to your news diet!).

8. Always ask yourself: "What's the bigger picture here?" If you can't answer that question (or the news source doesn't immediately make it clear), the article is probably not worth your time. Don't get caught up in the noise or the infighting.

9. Follow photojournalists on social media; they can add interesting perspectives because they're actually physically *in* the region they're reporting on.

THE EXPERT:

Jenna Lee is an American journalist, writer, producer, and founder of Leep Media LLC and SmartHERNews.com. Prior to launching her own news business, she coanchored a daily two-hour news program for the Fox News Channel, where she reported on the biggest domestic and international stories of the last decade.

THE EXPLANATION:

Being thoughtful about where you go for your news is critical to ensure that you're getting information you can trust. Journalists matter, and a good journalist will cut down the amount of time you set aside to seek answers because they will provide you with a complete story, not a biased story. Likewise look for an editorialist who makes you think differently about any number of issues that may be of conversation—then you have your facts, but you also have an interesting point of view that you can discuss with other people. And before you invest the time in reading *anything*, think about the big picture. The news is often fueled by chasing the play-by-play, rather than explaining why a story or topic really matters. Finally, always leave yourself some time to focus on "good" news in the form of innovation—what is one cutting-edge technology you should know about or one new study that's challenging the way we think about our health or improving our lives? Finding something new to learn about reminds you to look over the headlines toward the horizon, and the endless exciting possibilities ahead.

Bonus

Try a newswire app. The Associated Press, for example, is an international wire service, so you can get a sampling of what's happening all over the world. And for the most part, it's dedicated to nonpartisan news delivery, which will help you stay focused (when the news isn't mixed in with editorials, it's easier to absorb what you need and move on).

A word about being informed:

"No matter how you feel politically, you're a citizen of a nation. I think it's an important duty to know what's happening; what are some of the big topics for the country. In many ways, keeping current is a great way to practice your patriotism. A little bit of information, on a regular basis, about the nation in which you live enriches your life in so many ways." —Jenna Lee

Pro tip: "If there are times when you're feeling particularly anxious about the state of the world, take a moment to separate your news consumption from your social media consumption. We know these two intersect, but reading one quality news article on a current event topic will be a better use of your time than stumbling across a news item with no context on social media. Intentional news consumption will actually *lower* anxiety, and heighten your awareness. Think quality over quantity—it's an oldie but a goodie for a reason!" —Jenna Lee

··· 2 ···

GET FROM POINT A TO POINT B

GET OUT THE DOOR IN THE MORNING (CALMLY AND WITHOUT FORGETTING ANYTHING)

"The space between putting on your shoes and backing out of your driveway is not zero. So many people think it is and that's why they're five minutes late everywhere."

—Laura Vanderkam

1. Designate a place to house all the things you need to take with you for your day—this could be a mudroom, a foyer, or the hallway by your front door.
2. Make sure everyone in the house knows about this place (give everyone their own hooks/bin/cubby for their coats, bags, shoes, etc.).
3. Anything belonging in this place that is found elsewhere needs to be immediately returned to that place, ideally by the person responsible for its migration (how else will they learn?).
4. Designate one bag or wallet for the important stuff you always need. If you remove anything from there, take the 8.5 seconds to return it. Do it now—I'll wait here.
5. Transport less stuff in general. What do you *really* need? Edit, edit, edit.

6. If there are things you often forget, get *two* of those things and leave one in the place you always need it. Have a gym at work? Keep an extra pair of sneakers under your desk. It's not a huge investment and it means you'll never forget.

7. Keep certain things in your car or your travel bag—an extra umbrella, reusable grocery bags, a spare pair of sunglasses. If you take these items out, put them back in. (Sensing a trend here?)

8. Group things together to force you to remember them. If you don't want to forget, say, the leftovers you packed for lunch, put your keys in the fridge on top of your chicken salad the night before.

9. If there's something really important you need to remember, write yourself a note and tack it somewhere you're guaranteed to look before walking out the door (on the door itself, perhaps).

10. Take a beat and mentally run through a checklist of what you need to take with you today.

THE EXPERT:

Laura Vanderkam is a time-efficiency expert and author of *Off the Clock: Feel Less Busy While Getting More Done*, *What the Most Successful People Do Before Breakfast*, and *168 Hours: You Have More Time Than You Think*. (Her hack for making sure her kids never forget their lunchboxes: They all buy school lunch!)

THE EXPLANATION:

Yes, a peaceful exit really starts with training yourself to put things back where they belong. Creating a home for those things means when you (or someone you live with) says, "Hey, where's my X?!" there's only one place it can be. And that happens to be right by the exit so you *have* to see them when you're leaving. People often say, "Get ready the night before and you'll save time in the morning."

But then you're actually taking *more* time because you're essentially getting ready twice. Not only that, you wind up staying up later at night because you still want some me time after all that prepping for the next day. Then getting to bed later makes the morning crappier, no matter what you do. Instead, figure out how to give everything a home so it's not that you have to put everything in its place the night before; it's that this stuff never leaves its place in, well, the first place. Anything you always need should be *in* something that always goes with you. (Keep your cash, cards, bus pass, sunglasses in the same wallet or bag—when you start switching back and forth between bags, that's when the "Oh &#!@, my driver's license is in the other one!" happens.) The things you're most likely to forget are the things you *can* leave at home, so group them with something you *can't* get out the door without (keys, say, or your pants). Well-placed notes can help, and if you have kids, post a weekly calendar of their activities right by the door so you can glance at it. But if you have so many things to actively remember in the morning that you require a full written checklist, your life may be too complicated! Pare back.

NAVIGATE A FOUR-WAY STOP

1. Come to a complete stop.
2. Be sure your signal is on if you're planning to turn.
3. Make eye contact with the other drivers.
4. Whichever car got there first goes first (this is basic etiquette, and it applies at intersections, too).
5. But wait, two people arrived at the same time? The car farthest to the right goes first. If three cars arrive at the same time, the car farthest to the right still goes first, then you go clockwise from there (meaning the car farthest to the left has to wait until both of the other cars have passed).

6. When two cars arrive at the same time and they're head-to-head, and one of the vehicles is turning and the other intends to go straight, the car going *straight* has the right of way. If both are going straight (i.e., their blinkers aren't blinking) or both are turning in opposite directions, proceed at the same time but slowly—you never know if the other driver is actually going to do what they've indicated.

7. If four cars arrive at the same time, there's no rule—you just wait for the most aggressive driver (there's always at least one!) to make the first move and then proceed *with caution* using the steps above.

THE EXPERT:

Emily Stein is the president of Safe Roads Alliance, a nonprofit dedicated to educating drivers to be safer on the roads. They work extensively in Massachusetts and across the United States to increase public awareness of distracted driving. Safe Roads Alliance publishes *The Parent's Supervised Driving Program*, a free guide for parents of teen drivers.

THE EXPLANATION:

Yes, you really need to stop at a stop sign—even if you're in a rush, even if there are no other cars there. If there *are* other cars, eye contact is crucial. You want to make the other drivers know you see them and they see you. This is an important safety check, especially when so many drivers are distracted. Even if drivers are using hands-free technology, when people are on their phones—and you know they are—they're not fully paying attention to the road. (And there are plenty of drivers who don't signal or signal the wrong way.) If you see a car stopped at a crosswalk you're approaching the first thing you have to do is think, *Pedestrians.* "Scan the street for wheels and feet" is a phrase to help you remember that we share the road with people walking and bicycling. If someone is in the crosswalk, drivers must yield to them. Common courtesy goes a long way while driving and can really make or break a person's commute. (Isn't it lovely when you let someone out in front of you and they give you that appreciative wave? Isn't it $*&@! annoying when they don't let *you* out or don't wave?!) Kindness can backfire, of course, if everyone is feeling generous that day and you're all waving each other to go first. When you have the "you go no you go no *you* go," just have a little laugh, bring some levity to the situation, and move on—someone, *anyone*, move on!

Bonus

What about the rotaries/roundabouts? As you're approaching, slow down and yield to the car on the *left*—meaning if someone is approaching the rotary from the left, and you do not have time to get in, *you* have to wait. If someone is already *in* the rotary, *they* have the right of way (meaning don't expect them to slow down so you can sneak in). If you're the car in the rotary, DO NOT stop to let others in; that is not your job, it's not the "nice" thing to do, and it can lead to real problems. One way to make roundabouts easier to navigate: Signal your intention. If you're in the rotary but you're going three-quarters of the way around, put on your left blinker to indicate that you're not coming out yet. It communicates to the drivers who are waiting that they shouldn't cut in front of you. When you *are* ready to exit, *indicate* it by putting on your right blinker.

Pro tip: Studies show that engaging with your phone in the car in any way (even a hands-free phone call) is cognitively distracting and, thus, impairs our driving. Even glancing at your phone at a red light can cause a "hangover effect," where the mind stays distracted for up to twenty-seven seconds before coming back to the present situation (i.e., those cars whizzing by you at 60 mph). As they say, hands free is not risk free.

PUMP YOUR OWN GAS

1. Know what side of the car your tank is on. (Hint: Look at the gas gauge on your dashboard. There's a little icon of a gas pump with an arrow next to it that points to the side it's on. MIND. BLOWN.)

2. Pull into the station on the appropriate side, and pull up so your tank is in front of the pump, leaving a few feet of walking room between them.

3. Release the fuel door *before* you get out of the car.

4. Shut off the engine and grab your credit or debit card and get out of your car to pay. (If you want to pay cash, you'll have to walk inside and estimate how much gas you'll be getting.)

5. Unscrew the cap on your gas tank (don't take this step until you're ready to pump).

6. Choose the fuel you want to use and push the button associated with it, then remove the nozzle from the pump (you may need to lift the lever as well) and insert it into your gas tank. Make sure it's all the way in, then rest the handle in place.

7. Depress the handle to start pumping. To keep the fuel flowing freely, locate the tiny clasp near the handle and fold it down so you can place it in the notches below it.

8. When the tank is full—you'll hear it stop—pull out the nozzle with the tip *up* so it doesn't drip. Then return the nozzle to the holder (if you needed to flip a lever before beginning, put it back down at this point).

9. Replace your fuel cap and make sure it's tight (listen for three clicks or, if yours doesn't click, tighten until it stops abruptly).

10. Collect your receipt, get back in your car, and slowly pull away from the pump.

THE EXPERT:

Chris Riley is the founder of AutoWise, an online community of car experts offering the latest news, insider insight, and how-tos for car enthusiasts around the world (and regular folks who just drive regular cars).

THE EXPLANATION:

Making this pit stop efficient is about checking things off the list *before* you even open your car door. Did you pop your tank? Did you shut off your engine? Do you have your credit card in your hand? That way you're not having to go back and forth five times. Just wait until you're really ready to pump to take off the gas cap—when it's removed, your tank is leaking fuel vapors into the atmosphere, which is no bueno for the environment. The hardest part of pumping gas is having to stand there and wait while the tank fills. You shouldn't go far but you can check your fluids and make sure they don't need to be topped off—or use the window wash tools to clean your windshield. And when you're ready to leave, proceed with caution. There will be people backing up and maneuvering because they forgot which side their tank is on (me, every single time I went to the gas station before writing this book).

Bonus

A few don'ts:

- **Don't** ever smoke around gas pumps. This should go without saying, but here it is anyway: Fuel is flammable and it doesn't take much to create a disaster.
- **Don't** use your cell phone while fueling. It's not likely, but there's a chance a spark might lead to a fire or even an explosion. Plus, being on your phone is a distraction you don't need—you might put in the wrong fuel or forget to replace your cap. (Some states even have laws against using your phone at the pump.)

- **Don't** reenter your vehicle while it's fueling. If you need to get inside for some reason, make sure you touch the metal frame of your car to discharge all the static electricity.

Fun fact: New Jersey is the only state left where it's illegal to pump your own gas.

JUMP-START A CAR

1. Find the battery in both the running car and the dead car (it's usually under the hood but can be in the trunk or under a seat).
2. Park the running car next to the dead car so that it's close enough for the jumper cables to reach both batteries, but with enough space to work, then shut it off.
3. Separate cables so you have one red and one black handle on each side; lay them on the ground near each battery. Don't let handles touch from this point on.
4. Find the positive and negative leads on each battery. The lead is the little bolt or knob on the top or side of the battery—the positive will have a "POS" or "+" on it and is usually red; the negative will have a "NEG" or "–" on it and is usually black.
5. Starting with the dead car, attach the red handle to the positive lead.
6. Moving to the good car, attach the other red handle to the positive lead, and the black handle to the negative lead.
7. Go back to the dead car and clamp the last black handle to the negative lead on the battery.
8. Start the working car and let the engine run for about a minute.
9. Start the dead car. (Feel free to cross your fingers first.)
10. Leaving both cars running, carefully disconnect the jumper cables in the reverse order they were connected: unclamp the

black handle from the jumped car, then the black and red handles from the other car and then the red handle from the jumped car. Do not let the clamps touch until they are all disconnected.

THE EXPERT:

Harry Hendrickson is the owner of Hendrickson Car Care in Halesite, New York, where he's been a beloved mechanic for more than fifty years. He's lost count of how many cars he's jumped but says it's a daily occurrence.

THE EXPLANATION:

This is one of those tasks where the order matters so much that if you don't follow it, sparks will fly—and not the good kind. If you let the positive and negative clamps touch while the other ends of the cables are connected to a battery, it will "arc," meaning electricity is passing through and it can melt the metal (and it will create sparks). And you don't want sparks near the engine because, well, gas fumes. (This is also why Harry says you shouldn't smoke while jumping a car—noted!) You start by clamping the red handle to the dead battery because that one has the least juice and is therefore the safest. Remember, red to red; black to black (connecting the cables wrong could cause the car's computer to short). And be sure your connections are secure by twisting on the handles a little and that the cables are out of the way before starting the cars. I mean you might just want to tear out this page and keep it in your glove compartment. I won't be offended.

Pro tip: If the jump works and your car starts (if you have good jumper cables and you followed everything above, it should!), don't shut off your engine. Drive around or leave it running for at least thirty minutes to recharge your battery. If the car won't start the next time you use it, the battery needs to be replaced.

··· **3** ···

WORK SMARTER

GET DRESSED FOR A BIG DAY AT WORK

"Think of planning your outfits like food prep—the more you can do ahead of time the less stress (and more success) you'll have when it comes time to put it all together."

—Sali Christeson

1. Plan your outfit at least one full day before your meeting or presentation (this may require running to the dry cleaner to pick something up, so don't wait until 6 p.m. the night before).
2. When in doubt, go with something you feel great in even if it's not the newest or fanciest thing you own.
3. Choose a color you love but also one that's flattering on you. (Don't know? Pay attention when your friends say, "Wow, that color looks great on you.")
4. If you'll be on a screen (Zoom, Skype, *Today* show interview), skip the patterns—they can be distracting—and avoid colors that wash you out. On camera, crimson generally looks great on most people.
5. Make sure all the important pieces are ironed or steamed. SEE PAGE 98 FOR HOW TO IRON A SHIRT.

6. Gather everything else you need to complete the look—jewelry, undergarments, shoes—and have it all hanging together in your closet.

7. In the morning, do as much as you can *before* getting dressed (hair, makeup, eating breakfast, feeding/kissing/even looking at kids). Don't risk makeup or child spillage on your top; throw on a T-shirt instead of your actual shirt.

8. Finish getting dressed right before you're ready to walk out the door.

9. Take a picture of yourself in the mirror (or ask someone who lives with you to do it) so you can remember this look the next time you're trying to figure out what to wear.

10. Walk out the door. SEE PAGE 200 FOR HOW TO WALK INTO A ROOM WITH CONFIDENCE.

THE EXPERT:

Sali Christeson is the founder and CEO of Argent, an emerging fashion brand at the forefront of the workwear revolution. (Prior to launching Argent, Sali spent a decade in the finance and technology industries, where she struggled to find clothes that looked good but were also practical and professional.) Argent's blazers have hidden pockets on the inside to hold phones, credit cards, hand sanitizer, you name it. Clients include Hillary Clinton, Kamala Harris, Amy Poehler, and America Ferrera.

THE EXPLANATION:

Make all the decisions beforehand so on the morning of your big day at work, you can focus on your presentation/interview/event and not on what the $!#!&! you're gonna wear. On average women waste twenty to thirty minutes—and sometimes up to an hour—trying on different outfits. Not productive! Don't forget to locate the underwear and bra you need for that particular outfit, too. And knowing what color profile works best with your complexion is important because you want colors that make you pop. It will help you look bold and confident, and help people remember you. Of course the key to making this run smoothly is actually *liking* the options you have in your closet. You may want to purchase something new for the occasion. Most workwear companies have stylists whose job it is to help you find clothes that work for you, your body type, your industry. They'll take a bunch of Polaroids and give you a ton of different outfit combinations so you can see how it translates in real life.

Bonus

The staples every woman should have in her closet (to help make the getting-ready portion of the day faster...and expletive free):

- a really good-quality tailored suit—pants and blazer—that you can wear as is or mix and match (the blazer over a jumpsuit; the pants with a denim jacket)
- a nice pair of office-appropriate jeans (especially in light of the modern workplace shifting toward casual)
- basic black pants
- a blazer (in a different color than the suit)
- a denim jacket (and maybe a leather jacket, too)
- a good trench coat

Err on the side of quality over quantity—these are "investment pieces" that will become the foundation of your wardrobe. Then you periodically buy new blouses and tank tops and scarves and accessories for less money to keep your staples feeling fresh.

SIT PROPERLY IN YOUR CHAIR

1. Stand up tall in front of your chair.
2. Ground your feet, finding the inside and outside parts and rooting them to the ground.
3. Engage your core and then bend your knees to sit down while keeping your upper body as tall as you can (core strength helps here).
4. Once you're sitting, focus on your pelvis and shift your sitz bones around until you're comfortable.
5. Lean forward a little to stack your torso directly over your pelvis.
6. Shrug your shoulders to your ears, and pull them back then down.
7. Lift your head up and back so it's held high and in line with your pelvis and torso.
8. Position your chair so your hips are either above or level with your knees, so knees are at 90-degree angles or more.

THE EXPERT:

Steven Weiniger is an internationally renowned posture expert and author of *Stand Taller—Live Longer: An Anti-aging Strategy*.

THE EXPLANATION:

Having good posture means less stress on your muscles and joints, but studies also show that people who have slumped-over posture have higher levels of cortisol (the stress hormone) and lower levels of testosterone. Not to mention the vibe you put out when you're hunched over. Standing—and sitting—tall makes you appear more confident and put together. So the first step to sitting properly is to *stand* properly. You build good posture from the ground up so focus on your feet, then your pelvis, then your torso, then your head. When people sit down the first thing they do is slump forward.

Making sure your hips are never below your knees helps prevent that (this may mean adjusting your chair height). When you're sitting properly, your hands should lay comfortably on the desk, your arms making right-ish angles at your elbows. Will you forget this posture when you get focused on whatever you're doing? Yes, but if you can remember to check in and reset yourself even a few times a day it makes a big difference. And the straighter you sit, the more you're engaging your core (six-pack, here we come!).

Bonus

No matter how properly you sit, try to get up and move often throughout the day. General guidelines say about every thirty minutes. Think of work habits you can create to keep you moving (walking meetings, for example) because the body wasn't meant to be sitting as much as we do.

SEND AN EFFECTIVE EMAIL

"One of the main reasons people wind up working late is because they suck at writing emails."

—Justin Kerr

1. Use a simple subject line and keep it to seven words or less (it needs to fit on one line across a mobile phone screen for easy legibility).
2. Skip the long greeting. A simple "Hi, Nick" is all you need before getting to the point.
3. Start with your conclusion—that is, what you're hoping to get from this email.
4. Use bullet points to list action items needed. (Is it clear what you're asking of the recipient? Make sure your thoughts are organized to make it easy for them to say yes.)

5. Leave white space.
6. Check your formatting. What's the email going to look like for the recipient (i.e., when it's shrunk down to a 2-inch-by-4-inch screen)? A never-ending block of extra-large text feels overwhelming.
7. Delete anything superfluous and add more white space.
8. Pick a sign-off word ("best," "thanks," "regards") and stick with it.
9. Write your name (even if you skip a sign-off word); otherwise the email can feel a little dismissive, especially if you're asking the recipient to do something for you.
10. Delete any long signatures that include inspirational quotes, images, or your entire LinkedIn profile. (Signatures junk up people's inboxes, often come through as attachments, and otherwise make it hard for them to quickly read and reply.)

THE EXPERT:

Justin Kerr is a workplace efficiency consultant, creator of the *Mr. Corpo* podcast, and author of *How to Write an Email*, *How To Be Great at Work*, and *How to Cry at Work*.

THE EXPLANATION:

The purpose of an email is to get the information you need as quickly and as easily as possible. That starts with a straightforward subject line. Even if you're corresponding with a person about something else, when you're starting a conversation about a new topic start a new email chain with a new subject line; otherwise, the recipient is more likely to ignore it as it can appear to be old news. In grade school we're taught to do intro, supporting evidence, then conclusion. In work email it's the opposite: conclusion first, action steps, then supporting evidence (if they want to read that far down). The secret to really effective emails: bullet points. Think about the recipient's *experience* of your email. You may be writing it on a giant desktop or laptop screen, but people will probably be *reading* it on their iPhone between meetings or while getting out of an Uber. White space gives them breathing room and makes it easier to navigate and respond. For your sign-off, find a word that feels like you and always use that word—it's one less decision you have to make in your day à la Steve Jobs and his work attire (think of "regards" as your black turtleneck).

Bonus

If things start to get testy over email, don't respond. You can't win an email fight over email. Step away from the computer and solve the issue one-on-one, either over the phone or in person. The good news: Bullies usually shrink in the moment of confrontation. Say: "Hi, it looks like we have a disagreement." And they'll likely say, "Oh no, whatever *you* want...I was just making a comment." If it was a group email, it's important that you reply all with a resolution ("Hey, this was resolved, we're doing X") so everyone knows the potential for an email fight is over. This also gives you credibility as someone who solves problems...and wins email fights.

LEAVE A VOICEMAIL

"Rule of thumb: If your listener has to replay the message, you probably haven't done your job."

—Joel Schwartzberg

1. Think of yourself as speaking in bullet points, not paragraphs.
2. Practice out loud a few times (this will help condition your mind and mouth to work in unison).
3. When you hear the beep, start with a short salutation ("Hi, Sarah") and immediately identify yourself and your affiliation

("I'm Amy Smith from the ABC Corporation"). Do this *very* slowly, with emphasis on *articulation*.

4. Give your phone number up front.
5. If necessary, briefly note your connection to the listener: "We met at the corporate conference last week" or "I got your name from our mutual friend Kevin."
6. Avoid long prefaces like apologies (does saying "I'm so sorry to bother you with this" make it any less bothersome?) and get to your point immediately. Are you hoping to set up a meeting? Get an email address? Get paid? Say it.
7. Keep your ask very simple and clear, and make *only one request*.
8. Give your contact information again—slow down and overarticulate—then repeat it.
9. End with two things: Appreciation ("Thanks, Sarah") and an indication of what you want to happen next ("I look forward to talking/working/addressing this with you").

THE EXPERT:

Joel Schwartzberg is a strategic communications trainer and author of *Get to the Point! Sharpen Your Message and Make Your Words Matter*. He is also a professional speechwriter and National Champion public speaker who has written for *Harvard Business Review*, *Fast Company*, and *Toastmaster Magazine*.

THE EXPLANATION:

OK, so leaving voicemails is a little archaic (sorry, Dad), but sometimes it's necessary. Knowing what you're going to say is obviously key here. The bullet-point mind-set will help you focus on critical messages and cut unnecessary words (i.e., get to the point!). Multipart asks complicate the message, putting a burden on the listener who may have ears on you but eyes on Instagram—I mean, their work email. That's why you clearly say your name up front: If you rush this part, they may spend the rest of your voicemail thinking, *Wait, who is this?!* instead of paying attention to what you're saying. Most people wait until the end of a voicemail to leave their contact info, but if the recipient doesn't catch it the first time, they'll be forced to listen to the entire message again (soooooo annoying) so give your phone number or email (choose one form of contact info) up front, too.

INTRODUCE TWO PEOPLE OVER EMAIL

1. Put both people's names in the subject line: "Introducing Erin and Justin."
2. Address the email specifically to each person (if you're reaching out to one person on behalf of the other, address the person being *reached out to* first). "Erin, I wanted you to meet Justin."
3. Say something about Justin (and maybe share a link to his profile or website).
4. Address the person you're helping out: "Justin, Erin is the person I was telling you about." Add a line of context if it's needed to make it clear why you're connecting these people.
5. Direct them on who should do what next. "Justin, you should follow up with Erin and buy her a coffee."
6. Ask to be dropped to BCC or deleted from the chain. "No need to include me going forward."

THE EXPERT:

Justin Kerr is a workplace efficiency consultant, creator of the *Mr. Corpo* podcast, and author of *How to Write an Email*, *How To Be Great at Work*, and *How to Cry at Work*.

THE EXPLANATION:

Take the time to provide context—sharing their LinkedIn profiles or websites makes this easy—and be prescriptive for who should take the next step. That is often the biggest dilemma people face when being introduced over email: Who responds first? Your job as the person making the intro is to help them out with who should take charge of setting up a meeting/call/coffee. And asking to be dropped from the chain going forward is just being kind to your inbox.

MAKE YOUR POINT HEARD

"People won't remember the specific words you'll say, but they will remember what you meant . . . if you have a point."
—Joel Schwartzberg

1. Figure out what your point is (a point is an argument; it's not simply a theme or a topic). Ask yourself, "If my audience can take away only one idea from my communication, what would I want it to be?" This should spotlight your point.
2. To make sure your idea is indeed a point, run it through the "I believe that _____" litmus test. (Take what you think is your point and put it in the blank. If it makes a complete sentence you have a point; if it doesn't, rethink what you're trying to say.)
3. Make that point stronger by conveying the *single highest value proposition* (i.e., the "so what"). Instead of saying, "If we properly prepare for the meeting, we will impress the client and be able to better express our ideas and things will run more efficiently," say, "If we properly prepare for this meeting, we will win the business." Boom!
4. Avoid "badjectives" (adjectives so broad they convey no value). Instead of saying something is "great," say what *makes* it great.

This is the "why," and you need to articulate it in a way that has impact.

5. Get in and get out. Once you've made your point, zip it.

THE EXPERT:

Joel Schwartzberg is a strategic communications trainer and author of *Get to the Point! Sharpen Your Message and Make Your Words Matter.* He is also a professional speechwriter and National Champion public speaker who has written for *Harvard Business Review, Fast Company,* and *Toastmaster Magazine.*

THE EXPLANATION:

It may seem like a no-brainer to have a point before trying to make one, but you'd be surprised by how many people just talk and talk and expect the other person to be able to pick up what they're putting down. To have impact, you want to propose something of value, so honing your message is essential. As is editing yourself, especially with adjectives like *excellent, fantastic,* or *great*—they're deceptive (who wouldn't want to be connected to something excellent?), but they're not really saying anything. Most of us know "less is more," but we also need to understand "more is less." If you have multiple thoughts to convey, don't jam them into a single point. Pick the most important one, focus on it, and bring up the others later, one at a time. And don't ramble. People remember the last thing you said, so going on and on at the end will only dilute and distract from your point.

GIVE SOMEONE CONSTRUCTIVE FEEDBACK

1. Ask the person for permission and/or time to give them feedback. "Hey, I'm wondering if I can give you a piece of feedback, would that be OK?"

2. State your intention (*why* you're giving them feedback). Before you start, make sure that you're clear with the intention yourself—it shouldn't be to embarrass or degrade the person, only to help them be more successful.

3. Name what you're observing—this is the "what," and it should be objective, morally neutral, and quantifiable.[2]

4. Tell them how what you observed compares to what the norm is. This is the "what compared to what" step. If you haven't communicated the norm ahead of time, now's the time to say, "Here's what's expected."

5. Share the impact of their behavior—the "so what." This ensures that person understands the impact this change will have and can focus on that.

6. Put the behavior in context, the "what I know about you" step. "One of the things I know about you is that you care deeply about our client, so I'd like you to consider making a change that I think may better reflect that."

7. Ask, "What do you think?"

8. Come up with an action plan, the "now what?" Ideally it will be collaborative, but if not, it should come more from *them* than from you.

9. Thank them. Being able to receive feedback is a behavior you want to reinforce, so if they do it and do it well, let them know.

---

2. If you're giving feedback to someone who's receptive to feedback, cares about the quality of their work, and cares about their relationship with you, you may not need to go any further than this step. They may say, "Got it, thank you, I'm gonna work on that."

THE EXPERT:

Deborah Grayson Riegel is the CEO and chief communication coach for Talk Support, an executive coaching firm focused on leadership and communication skills. She has taught for the Wharton School at the University of Pennsylvania, Columbia Business School, and Duke Corporate Education. She is the author of *Overcoming Overthinking: 36 Ways to Tame Anxiety for Work, School, and Life.*

THE EXPLANATION:

If you're the boss, you don't have to ask permission to give feedback. You should, however, set the stage to ensure you're giving feedback in a way that will resonate and lead to quick and productive change. So you could say, "Would this be an OK time to give you some feedback on that client meeting?" And your intention could be something like "I think it will help you serve our customer better." Then go to the six essential steps:

1. "What"—Make sure the "what" is about a behavior, not their personality or character. Say "In our meeting I saw you interrupt our client three times" instead of "You were being rude to the client." (Rude is an interpretation, you can't see rude; you can see interrupting.)
2. "What compared to what"
3. "So what?"
4. "What I know about you"—In order for constructive feedback to not be taken totally negatively, you can put the feedback in the context of positive things you know about that person.
5. "What do you think?"—Hopefully this will have felt like a dialogue rather than a monologue, so the "What do you think?" might have come earlier—but if it didn't, make sure you get to it. Say "I've been talking for a while now, and this is my perspective. What's yours? Where do we overlap and where do we not?"

6. "Now what?"—Put a date on the calendar to check in on this again. When we give someone feedback—a child, a spouse, an employee—we often think, *OMG, I hope I don't have to bring this up again, ugh!* Take that dread and anxiety out of the equation by *planning* to bring it up again.

RUN A PRODUCTIVE MEETING

1. Make sure you're crystal clear on the purpose of the meeting; then ask yourself: "Is this meeting necessary?" If yes...
2. Pick a good venue. If you have the same old boring meeting in the same old boring place, you'll get the same old boring results.
3. Think through who needs to attend and *confirm that they will.* You can't always trust an accepted calendar invite.
4. Make the purpose of the meeting clear to all who will be attending so they can show up prepared.
5. Plan how the meeting will run—not just the bulleted agenda, but the *process* for each item: Is this one requiring blue-sky ideas, so we'll brainstorm? Are we making a decision here? Is it just FYI?
6. Decide how the meeting will be documented, to what level of detail and by whom.
7. Start on time. ON. TIME.
8. If your meeting will be longer than, say, two hours, let people know there will be breaks. People are less likely to be distracted on their phones if they know there will be a chance to check them at the break.
9. Give everyone next steps and be clear about who will do what by when. Define what "done" looks like for each of the to-do items so that everyone has similar expectations about that.
10. End on time. Or, if you really want people to be happy, a little early.

THE EXPERT:

Rebecca Sutherns, Ph.D., is the founder of Sage Solutions, a consulting firm that specializes in collaborative strategic planning (among other things, Rebecca goes into businesses and teaches them how to prepare for—and facilitate—successful meetings). Her latest book is *Nimble, Off Script But Still On Track*.

THE EXPLANATION:

You don't need meetings for the sake of meetings. What's the minimal viable format for the discussion at hand—could it be a phone call? an email? a conference call? (The main reasons to hold an in-person meeting are to reduce blind spots and increase everyone's buy-in.) Really homing in on the purpose can help you decide if the meeting is even worth holding, and then keep the group on track throughout. (If you don't know what "on track" is, you're more likely to meander off of it!) Too many people are invited to meetings they don't need to attend, and we've all been at meetings where people say, "Oh, I can't make a decision on that. I have to ask so-and-so," so make sure the invite list is on point (and that "so-and-so" is there). And people think more creatively when they're in creative spaces—those can be inside or outside the office; its more about changing it up than it is about the features of the space itself, although both are important. If you can manage the details and the clarity of the meeting well, people will be really engaged. (Visuals help people stay interested and retain the information as well.) Finally, what gets written down is what lives on after the meeting, so be sure that documentation happens and that it's accurate and not so long and awful that no one reads it.

Pro tip: When the meeting is over, it's over. No need to stick around chitchatting. If you're an attendee you can ask "Do we have everything we need from me today?" If the answer is yes, go. No need to tell them *why* you don't want to linger or what's so pressing (um, your job!), and definitely don't say you're just *soooo* busy (it makes it sound like you're more important than other people and other people don't like that).

LEAVE A WORK FUNCTION EARLY

1. Before you go, make your case internally about *why* you're going (and why it's OK to duck out).
2. Manage expectations—your own and everyone else's—by letting the key people know your plan.
3. Don't check your coat.
4. Front-load your networking.
5. Say your thank-yous and good-byes; don't just duck and leave.
6. Walk out without guilt. Your being there was a win for you and a win for them.
7. Use the time between leaving the event and getting home to decompress. Take some deep breaths, finish up on emails, jot down some notes, or do something to help yourself transition out of the previous activity and get ready for what's next.

THE EXPERT:

Lauren Smith Brody is the founder of the Fifth Trimester consulting, which helps businesses retain female talent by supporting new parenthood in the workplace, and author of *The Fifth Trimester: The Working Mom's Guide to Style, Sanity, and Success After Baby.*

THE EXPLANATION:

Owning your decision is the most important step to a successful duck-out, so in your head debate why you want to go and what you'll get from being there. Prepare yourself that you may have to leave in the middle of something good, and prepare your coworkers that there will be an empty seat at the table when dessert is served. When you actually arrive, set yourself up for an easy exit (e.g., don't sit in the middle of a row of seats; sit on an aisle). You want to get the most out of the time that you have, so go for face time, and make sure you see the people you need to see (maybe even get there a little early). It can be hard to walk into a small group and introduce yourself, but let the fact that your time is limited embolden you. Just don't get sidelined with one person who may not be the most important person to talk to but is the most *comfortable* person to talk to (e.g., your work bestie). And not ghosting is key. It may be a whisper and a nod, a bear hug, or even a quick chat to say you're so glad you came, what you got out of it, and that you can't wait to hear how the rest of it goes tomorrow.

Pro tip: "If you're leaving because you're a working parent, then when you get home (or the following morning) tell your child where you were, what you were doing, and why it was important for you to be there. You should feel comfortable bringing your parenthood into the workspace but also bringing the work home to your family so kids understand that you don't just disappear in a poof every day. You don't have to hide the fact that you work, why you work, nor the challenges and the victories. They help make you a whole person, and that's good for kids to see." —Lauren Smith Brody

ASK FOR A RAISE

1. Think about the raise you want, and remember: It's not just about money. More flexibility? More vacation days? More responsibilities or a title change?
2. Identify your walkaway (i.e., the lowest you'll accept). That may be your current salary or it may be higher if you have

something else to go to. Think about talking to HR to see if your compensation is fair before you go into this conversation. Also research the average in the market for your salary, define your bold aspiration, and figure out where you will anchor the negotiation. Your anchor is how much you will actually ask for, which should be higher than your aspiration so you have room to haggle.

3. Have something else to go to—another job offer, a role in another department, or even a meeting with HR to see if there are other opportunities in the department, division, or company.

4. Think about what's important to your supervisor and what he or she may need.

5. Find the right time to get on your supervisor's calendar—and tell her what the meeting is about. (Do not blindside her in the hallway to ask for a raise.)

6. Begin the negotiation by saying something like, "I'd like to talk about a raise and a few other things that are important to me, but I also hope to talk about what's important to you and how we can come up with something that works for both of us."

7. Discuss some of the things you identified in step 4. Maybe your boss does a lot of networking that keeps her out late and away from her family. You could offer to take on some of that responsibility.

8. Eventually she'll say, "OK, how much are you asking for?" Now is when you put together your story of how much you're worth, what you do well, why you're so great, and what you want (your anchor).

9. If it appears your boss isn't going to say yes, bring up step 3. "The reason this is so important to me is that I have another offer. I want to stay here, so I'd love to work with you to figure out how we can make that happen."

THE EXPERT:

Tad Mayer is the president of Career Negotiations, where he coaches individuals and corporations on leadership progress, employee engagement, and individual advancement (i.e., how to get that raise).

THE EXPLANATION:

The more prep you do the better this conversation will go. If you pop into your supervisor's office asking for "more" or "a bump," it will probably not be as much as you want. Having another job offer is obviously huge as it gives you leverage—just use it as a point of information, not a threat. And don't lead with your awards and accolades; instead focus the conversation on what you can do for the other person. She's still not going to be excited to have the conversation, but the idea is to get her engaged so that *she* will eventually ask *you* what *you* want. Whoever meets the other person's needs best (or has the best alternative to do something without the other person) has the most power in the negotiation. If you can give her something she needs, she'll be more compelled to come to an agreement with you.

CHAPTER

··· **4** ···

HAVE A PRODUCTIVE WORKDAY

ORGANIZE YOUR WORKDAY

"Balance is as much about managing your attention as is it about managing your day. Creating a strong outline for a sustainable schedule not only allows you to catch your breath, it ensures that you're aware of *how* and *where* you're allocating your time."

—Nicole Lapin

1. Prioritize your to-do list by looking at what's already scheduled for the day and identifying nonnegotiables. FOR HOW TO WRITE A TO-DO LIST YOU'LL ACTUALLY CHECK OFF, SEE PAGE 78.

2. Procrastinate. Seriously! Put things that aren't time sensitive on the list for tomorrow (or later).

3. Look at which of the remaining tasks align with your goals and eliminate those that don't. Then rank the ones that are left in descending order of priority.

4. Eat the frog. Mark Twain supposedly said, "If it's your job to eat the frog, it's best to do it first thing in the morning. And if it's your job to eat two frogs, it's best to eat the biggest one first." In other words, check off the biggest or most dreaded tasks first.

5. Pay attention to your body clock and how you feel at different times of the day so you can plan your work accordingly

(e.g., tackle the more focus-oriented tasks when you're most clearheaded).

6. Schedule a block of time to answer emails or do "think work" in the morning, when you're most awake.

7. Plan meetings for after lunch. Research shows that the afternoon, especially 3 p.m., is the optimal time for social activities like meetings.

8. Don't schedule something for 30 minutes or an hour just because it looks organized on your calendar. (If a meeting should take only 7 minutes, boom! You just got 23 minutes of your life back.)

THE EXPERT:

Nicole Lapin is the author of *Becoming Super Woman: A Simple 12-Step Plan to Go from Burnout to Balance*. She was the youngest-ever anchor on CNN before holding the same title at CNBC, anchoring the network's early-morning show, while covering business topics for MSNBC and *Today*. She's also the author of *Rich Bitch* and *Boss Bitch*.

THE EXPLANATION:

Creating a productive plan for the day is all about prioritizing, which necessarily means putting some things off until tomorrow or later. And always take your natural rhythms into consideration when planning your day. Your brain is the sharpest it's going to be within the first two to four hours of waking up. When it comes to prioritizing, putting off and stressing about the thing you're dreading only gives it more of your brain's real estate. So if you have to fire someone, take accountability for something, or tackle an intimidating project, do it early and get it over with. And determine whether holding that meeting in person is something you need to do, or if it would be more time effective over the phone (or on Zoom). SEE PAGE 50 FOR HOW TO RUN MORE EFFICIENT MEETINGS.

A word about being busy:

" 'Busy' people fill in their schedule indiscriminately: organizing your desktop, picking up dry cleaning, grabbing drinks with an acquaintance whom you have no real interest in seeing. 'Productive' people prioritize their tasks in accordance with their goals and emotional wellness needs. Pay close attention to what you do with your day and put thoughtful intention into how you fill your schedule." —Nicole Lapin

STAY ON TOP OF YOUR EMAIL INBOX

"Email is our common language and is still the single most important form of communication in offices."

—Justin Kerr

1. Get to work 10 minutes early.
2. Review and answer all new emails before your meetings start.
3. Keep outgoing messages short and to the point. SEE PAGE 41 FOR HOW TO WRITE AN EMAIL.
4. Add people to an email only if they really need to be on it (this avoids being inundated with reply-all messages).
5. If someone put you on a group email, be sure you reply all so people know you're responsible.
6. When you're asking someone for something, give them odd deadlines (Tuesday at 3:22 p.m.). This sets *your* deadline apart from all the others ("EOD Thursday" is the white noise of offices—plus, everyone's "end of day" means something different).
7. If you have a long thread going back and forth with someone that doesn't seem to be going anywhere, pick up the phone or go to their desk and solve it offline.

THE EXPERT:

Justin Kerr is a workplace efficiency consultant, creator of the *Mr. Corpo* podcast and author of *How to Write an Email*, *How To Be Great at Work*, and *How to Cry at Work*. He gives forty talks a year in corporate offices where he tells people they should be sending *more* emails, not less (they don't always believe him).

THE EXPLANATION:

Email is a game of staying ahead of the power curve. You've got to get emails out of your inbox so people can get *you* the information you need to keep moving forward. Whatever your schedule is like, find secret five-minute windows throughout the workday. Use them to answer one or two emails (these little spurts of productivity can add up to thirty minutes or more a day). If you're put on a group email, yes, you need to reply all—you may think you're helping people by just responding to the person who sent it, but you'll leave the others wondering about your buy-in and wasting time having to follow up. If you still feel like you're in the weeds, back up your start time by another ten minutes the next day. Continue to get in earlier by increments of ten minutes until you feel caught up and can reset. That means for a week or so you may have to get to work early—but the alternative is going the next six months feeling completely overwhelmed.

Bonus

Never send work emails on weekends or late at night. For one, it looks like you can't keep up with your job but, more important, if you answer emails at 11 p.m. or on Sundays, people will come to expect that level of accessibility. Oprah taught us that we teach people how we want to be treated. Teach people that you answer work emails only during work hours.

CREATE SECURE PASSWORDS (THAT YOU'LL ACTUALLY REMEMBER)

"A computer will calculate and recognize patterns a lot quicker than the human brain. But one thing humans are still better at is being creative—that's your great advantage over hacking tools!"
—the editors of MakeUseOf

1. Create a base password—start by thinking of a phrase, the name of a place, or a name and phone number.
2. Now make it less recognizable. You can take a phrase you love—"Love Makes The World Go Round"—and use the first letter of each word to create a new word: LMTWGR. Or randomly replace letters in a word with numbers (e.g., *Lifeskills* becomes *Lif3skill5*). Or reverse-spell your word (e.g., *Technology* becomes *ygolonhceT*).
3. Add numbers or special characters to it (change letters to specific numbers or symbols so you remember—*i* changes to *1* or *!*) or switch the spelling of known words (*love* becomes *luv*, *to* becomes *2*).
4. Make sure your base password meets the following criteria:

   - You can't find it in a dictionary.
   - It contains special characters and numbers.
   - It contains a mix of uppercase and lowercase letters.
   - It contains at least 10 characters.
   - It can't be easily guessed based on user information—your birthday, zip code, phone number, or the street you grew up on (whoops).

5. Commit that base password to memory. You can do it!
6. Once you have a strong base password, use it to create individual passwords for each of your online accounts by adding the

first three letters of the service to the end or the beginning of your base password, e.g., *passwordGma* for your Gmail account or *passwordeBa* for eBay. (Note: *Password* is not a good password.)

THE EXPERTS:

Tina Sieber and Yaara Lancet are technology writers and editors of MakeUseOf, an online guide that issues daily tips and guides on how to make the most of the internet, computer software, and mobile apps.

THE EXPLANATION:

Off the top of your head, how many different passwords do you have? If your answer is ten or less, you must be using the same password for different services, which puts you at risk.

The trick to remembering a large number of passwords is having a *base* password you can tweak according to the service you're signing in to. That way you're really only remembering one password. And you really do want to have individual passwords for every account. Imagine a hacker cracked that one password! Note that some accounts won't allow you to use special characters. In that case, you should increase the length and make the password as abstract as possible. Likewise, if the password length is limited to six or eight characters, make sure you cover as many of the other points as possible.

Bonus

Need help coming up with a good word for your base password? Choose a book you own in paper format, open it on a random page, or find a paragraph you especially like, and locate a word you can use. For example, in Charles Dickens's *Oliver Twist*, on page 109, there's the word *jocularity*. This is the fourth word on line 33 on this page, so the base password can be 109jocularity334. Play around with the numbers to place them in a way that's easier for you to remember. For good measure, you can add some symbols in a strategic place. You can even go ahead and mark the word in the book with a pencil, to make sure you can find it again if you happen to forget the password.

Pro tip: Use a password manager (a piece of software that can create almost uncrackable passwords and remember them for you). You just remember your single master password and all of your other passwords are stored securely for retrieval as and when you need them. They automatically fill log-in credentials with one click, so they're super convenient. Some can even store and autofill credit card details and billing addresses, which makes online shopping safer and more convenient.

Fun fact: Two of the most commonly used passwords are *password* and *123456*.

DECIDE WHAT TO EAT FOR LUNCH (SO YOU DON'T ZZZZZZ AT YOUR DESK)

1. List three places you're always in the mood to order from.
2. Ask yourself: "What do I know I like to eat there that generally makes me feel good?"
3. Narrow that down by thinking about what you had for your last meal or snack—if you ate just carrots and hummus, you may not be satisfied with a salad.
4. Consider what's on the menu for dinner and what time you'll be eating it. Aim for variety and make sure it's enough to keep you satiated (or not too much if dinner's early).
5. Look at your calendar to see what's on tap for the afternoon— big meeting? Skip the grains (which add extra carbs and can make you sleepier *just* when you need a pick-me-up!).
6. Think about how you can add more vegetables to your order based on the type of cuisine you chose (a side salad, an

extra vegetable roll, more spinach on the sandwich, veggie chili).

7. Add an unsweetened drink—hydration is key!

THE EXPERT:

Jaclyn London is a registered dietitian (RD) and certified dietitian-nutritionist and author of *Dressing on the Side (and other Diet Myths Debunked): 11 Science Based Ways to Eat More, Stress Less, and Feel Great About Your Body.* She previously served as Director of Good Housekeeping Institute's Nutrition Lab and is currently the head of Nutrition and Wellness for WW (formerly, Weight Watchers).

THE EXPLANATION:

We make less nutritious choices at work and a lot of that has to do with sheer volume—either it's not enough and we wind up grazing at the candy bowl, or it's too much and we want to crawl under our desks at 3 p.m. Being thoughtful about this stuff can set you up for a more productive afternoon. The goal is to get a combination of fiber, protein, and good-for-you fat. Fiber makes you feel full but also helps you slow down the rate at which you digest and absorb nutrients, creating a more steady release of glucose throughout your bloodstream—meaning you won't crash and burn. So get in more vegetables, more often, in whatever capacity you can (mind-set shift: think about what you can *add* to your meals, not what you should take away). Hydration is also key for energy, so keeping water or other unsweetened beverages handy helps. The good news: You can have more caffeine than you think—up to four hundred milligrams a day, which is four full eight-ounce cups of coffee!

Bonus

Ever feel like you've been drugged after a big, carb-heavy meal? There's a biochemical explanation for that. When you eat a lot of simple carbohydrates like those found in bread and pasta, your body releases insulin to deal with all the glucose and other smaller amino acids, and that leaves larger amino acids like tryptophan to go right to your brain without any competition. When tryptophan hits your brain it becomes serotonin and melatonin, which make you sleepy. If you're particularly prone to this—and many people are—skip the pasta and grains at lunch.

Fun fact: Turkey is not the cause of your post-Thanksgiving sluggishness. It's the heavy load of carbs found in pretty much everything else on the table. Turkey is particularly high in protein, which can actually *regulate* insulin levels and combat fatigue—so blame it on the stuffing, not the bird.

PREVENT (AND MANAGE) INTERRUPTIONS

1. Make an assertive request to be left alone for X amount of time.
2. Explain why you don't want to be interrupted. "I'm on a tight deadline and I'd love to have two hours to bang this out."
3. Don't be apologetic.
4. Ask for any obstacles that may arise. "Is there anything going on that would make honoring this request challenging or impossible for you?"
5. Express gratitude in advance.
6. Close your door, put on headphones, turn off notifications, and disconnect from all outside sources (you can even put an auto-response on your email and text messages) to signal to them and *yourself* that you're focused on something important.
7. Give and ask for feedback. After your period of peaceful work is over, find out how it impacted the people who allowed you to work. Hopefully it wasn't terrible, so you can use this trick again!

THE EXPERT:

Deborah Grayson Riegel is the CEO and chief communication coach for Talk Support, an executive coaching firm focused on leadership and communication skills. She has taught for the Wharton School at the University of Pennsylvania, Columbia Business School, and Duke Corporate Education. She is the author of *Overcoming Overthinking: 36 Ways to Tame Anxiety for Work, School, and Life*.

THE EXPLANATION:

Get ahead of interruptions by asking to be left alone, but be sure to say *why*—one of the fundamental ways we build trust with others is by explaining our decisions, even if the person doesn't necessarily agree with them. (If you need help explaining why you need this time, use this: Studies show that once concentration is broken it takes thirty minutes to get your flow back.) Your request shouldn't be aggressive or passive; it should be assertive. Aggressive is about getting your needs met at the expense of others' needs, passive is about getting other people's needs met at the expense of yours, and assertive is getting your needs met while still honoring the needs of someone else. So when you ask about obstacles that could arise, you may have to compromise or negotiate. But don't be reluctant to ask for the time that you need.

Bonus

When you inevitably get interrupted, try saying this: "I'm in the middle of something, you can have five minutes of my time now but please know that I'm distracted and you won't have my full attention. Or, you can have my full attention at X o'clock. Which do you prefer?" If they choose five minutes now, you have to honor it.

WORK FROM HOME

1. Designate a specific area for work (bonus points if there's a door you can close) so you're not just flopping on the couch with your laptop...like me, right now, as I write this sentence.
2. Don't jump into work as soon as you wake up; give yourself time to transition into your day.
3. Shower and get dressed (you don't have to wear a suit, but getting out of your pajamas helps you get into the right mind-set for work).
4. Clearly communicate to your team when you will be available and then *be available* during those times.
5. Take a lunch or a break, but let people know you're going to be away from your computer before you go.
6. Don't try to multitask and do housework; focus on your work during work hours.
7. Make time for human interaction (meet another WFH friend for coffee or a walk during your lunch break).
8. Create a time that you log off, just like at the office. Close that door from step one.
9. Don't forget about networking and career development—get into your actual office for face time when (and if) you can, attend conferences, set lunch meetings.

THE EXPERT:

Lauren McGoodwin is the author of *Power Moves*, and the founder and CEO of Career Contessa, a career site built inclusively for women. They help women cultivate successful careers through expert advice, interviews, one-on-one mentoring, and online, skills-based courses and resources. (Lauren founded Career Contessa in 2013 after experiencing a gap in career development resources for women.)

THE EXPLANATION:

A morning routine that you stick to will set the tone for the day and prevent you from overworking. (Believe it or not, working *too* much is a big issue for work-from-homers. When there's no clear start and end times, the lines between work and home get easily blurred.) Getting dressed is also a signal to anyone else in the house that you are, in fact, working. The designated work area further helps you separate your work life from your home life. Intentionally communicate about when you're working and when you're not. If you were in an office with other people and going to lunch, you'd probably get up and announce "I'm going to lunch," or "I have a bunch of meetings." You can do the same when you work from home (i.e., you don't have to take your phone with you to the bathroom just to show that you're actually working). Find opportunities for human interaction—both on the day-to-day (coffee with a friend) and in your work world (a networking event). Working from home can get lonely, as we all now know way too well; if you're the one remote employee and everyone else is in the office, make sure it's built into your contract that they fly you in once a month or once every two months. If everybody else is having face time and you're the odd man out, that's not good.

Bonus

Avoid FOND—Fear Of Not Doing. People experience FOND big-time when they're working from home because they feel like they have to be not just constantly working, but also multitasking. *Hey, I'm home, I should be doing the dishes and the laundry and running to the mailbox.* But getting distracted by your personal to-do list can be one of the biggest obstacles to effectively working from home. It takes discipline, but rather than taking a work break to put away laundry, take a break and go get lunch with a friend or walk to the park and let your brain rest, too.

Pro tip: If you have to leave a conference call or Zoom call early, and you know ahead of time, you can let the group know at the beginning. Say that you'll need to leave X minutes into the call and that you'll follow up after. When you need to leave, just hang up so you don't disturb people. If it's a sudden exit, it's best for you to announce it at the pause; just politely say you need to hop off but you'll follow up after. Then hop off! What's disruptive is when people take forever to say good-bye or expect good-byes from the rest of the group. Please, just go—quickly and quietly.

··· 5 ···

GET ORGANIZED AT HOME

DECLUTTER

"When you start to declutter a space, the problem is that you focus
on the stuff. But it's not about the stuff, it's about *you*."

—Peter Walsh

1. Ask yourself: "What's the vision I have for the life I want?"
2. Look at the space you're decluttering and the items you're considering and ask: "Does this thing help me create the life I want or does it distract me and *detract* from the life I want?"
3. Understand that there are two main types of clutter—"memory clutter" (reminds us of an important person, achievement, or event) and "I-might-need-it-one-day clutter" (a random piece of lumber, the fondue pot, your skinny jeans from college—the items we hold on to for all those imagined futures we might have).
4. Instead of thinking about what you want FOR a space (curtains, lamps, pillows, etc.) think about what you want FROM the space (comfort, escape, motivation, etc.).
5. Now that you're in the right headspace, give every person in the house two trash bags and set a timer for 10 minutes. Fill one with trash (or recycling) and the other with stuff to be donated.

Immediately place the trash items in the trash bin and take the donation bags to your car.

6. Employ the ratio rule: For items you have multiples of (books, toys, tees), pick a number between 1 and 10 and say for every X of these I keep, I'll get rid of 1. If you can't get your items to fit in the space you have for them, repeat the process (perhaps making X a little lower).

7. To declutter your kitchen, take everything out of your utensils drawers and leave those items in a cardboard box on your counter for a month. Every time you use something from the box, put it away where it belongs. At the end of the month take a look at what's left in the box and consider donating them. (Just remember to keep seldom-used but needed items like your turkey baster for Thanksgiving!)

8. For your closet, try the reverse hanger trick: Turn all items on hangers in your closet around the opposite way. Every time you wear something, hang the item back the correct way. At the end of six months, anything that hasn't been turned—except special occasion wear—gets donated. (You wear 20 percent of your clothes 80 percent of the time, and here's the proof!)

9. When decluttering a bathroom, read the numbers. Makeup has an expiration or a use-by date. A good rule of thumb: The closer the product is used to the eyes, the shorter the life span. Mascaras need to be replaced about every 4 months; other cosmetics and lotions can last up to a year. Perfume has a shelf life of 3 years.

THE EXPERT:

Peter Walsh is an organizational design expert, and television and radio personality. He's the author of numerous *New York Times* bestsellers including *It's All Too Much: An Easy Plan for Living a Richer, Fuller Life with Less Stuff* and *Let It Go: Downsizing Your Way to a Richer, Happier Life.*

THE EXPLANATION:

The first step is to rethink your relationship with your stuff—it should work *for* you, not the other way around. If it does, awesome, and if it doesn't, ask yourself: What is it doing in my home? We hold on to a lot of objects because we fear that if we let them go, we'll lose the memory or dishonor the person who gave them to us. Or we think we're going to need these things someday. But are you overwhelmed by this stuff? If it takes you out of the present, if you're anxious or preoccupied about what might happen in the future or are depressed and preoccupied with what happened in the past, you're not really living the best life you have *now*. That's where the decluttering comes in. All these tricks are meant to help you respect the space you have in your house so that you can truly be happy there.

ORGANIZE YOUR JUNK DRAWER

"Think of reorganizing your junk drawer as curating your own personal general store."

—Shira Gill

1. Clear off your kitchen counter so you have space to work.
2. Set a timer for 15 minutes.
3. Take everything out of the drawer and dump it on the counter.
4. Wipe down the drawer itself so all dust and debris (and melted cough drops?) are gone.
5. Identify what is actually junk—gum wrappers, old receipts, dried-out markers—and trash it.
6. Sort the rest of the stuff into two piles: One for things you want to put back in the drawer and one for things you want to keep but that belong elsewhere.

7. Install shallow drawer organizers—get a modular set and puzzle-piece it together based on what works for you and your stuff.

8. Put what you want to keep back in the drawer—this should be a very pared-down assortment of things you need frequent access to (Post-its, Sharpies, the extra garage clicker, gum, batteries).

9. Rebrand the drawer. If you call it a junk drawer, you're basically asking it to collect junk. So from now on refer to it as a *utility drawer.*

10. Relocate the other random things left on your counter to their rightful homes.

THE EXPERT:

Shira Gill is the founder of the popular home organization consultancy, Shira Gill Home, and author of *Minimalista*, forthcoming from Ten Speed Press in 2021.

THE EXPLANATION:

The timer is a trick Shira uses with clients to show them that this doesn't have to be a major project—overhauling your junk drawer can be a fifteen-minute makeover, something Shira has dubbed a "fifteen-minute win." (On Instagram she uses #15minwin to help her clients, and others around the globe, accumulate and celebrate their own little wins.) She also says that she typically finds that 90 percent of what's in a junk drawer is truly junk. So give yourself some tough love when it comes to the what-to-save step. That broken Christmas ornament you keep meaning to crazy-glue even though it has zero sentimental value? *Really?* The drawer organizers are important—one space for pens and pencils, one for scissors, one long one for your hammer (Shira keeps simple tools in her utility drawer!). You want to set up the drawer so it looks like a store both for easy access to your essentials and because it gives people pause before tossing crap in when they see how thoughtfully and lovely it's laid out.

OPEN YOUR MAIL

"You only want to touch mail twice: Once when you take it out of the mailbox and separate it and the second time when you're ready to deal with it for good. Don't open something 'just to see'—it's a waste of time and mental energy."

—Corinne Morahan

1. Identify *one* spot where mail goes (a corner of the kitchen counter, a tray on a console by the front door) and *one* spot where mail gets dealt with, like a desk in your home office (the place where you dump it and deal with it can be the same).
2. Get your mail every day, but only when you have at least two minutes.
3. Immediately separate the *unopened* mail into two categories: STAY and GO.
4. Put anything that stays in the "dumping spot" from step 1.
5. Toss anything that goes into either the trash can or recycling bin.
6. When you have 15 minutes to dedicate to opening the mail, either daily or weekly, take it to the place you designated to deal with it, and grab your calendar, phone, and/or laptop.
7. Open your mail!
8. If you get an invitation: Check your calendar, RSVP, mark your calendar, and toss the invitation (bonus points if you order the gift then, too—your future self will thank you!).
9. When you open a bill: Schedule the payment right then. SEE PAGE 80 FOR MORE ON BILL PAYING.
10. If it's a card: Read it, text a thank-you, chuck it, or file it.
11. Make a note in your calendar for any pending items you really can't deal with immediately, and leave them in the place you deal with mail.

THE EXPERT:

Corinne Morahan is the founder and CEO of Grid + Glam, a Boston-based full-service professional organizing company that marries aesthetics with functionality (her Instagram features drool-worthy desk and pantry makeovers). She created the G+G membership to give members the step-by-step tools, lessons, and resources to transform their own homes.

THE EXPLANATION:

The key to staying on top of mail is realizing that it's a daily chore, like doing the dishes. There are two parts to the process: physically gathering the mail and then dealing with it, which are often done at separate times. Going to the mailbox only when you have a few minutes to actually sort the mail is an important step—don't just grab it as you're flying to your car (bills *will* fall between the seats; trust me on this one). And be ruthless with that toss pile—yes, the catalogs are pretty, but they will just stack up and taunt you. And your time is worth more than the dollar you'll save uncovering the one perfect deal in all those coupons.

Bonus

Put a hold on your mail at the post office website if you're traveling for more than five days. Have it delivered the day *before* you're set to arrive home so it's waiting for you. The day you get home, follow steps 3, 4, and 5 above. Wait for step 6 until you have a least forty-five minutes to devote to it.

REORGANIZE YOUR DRAWERS AND CLOSET

1. Grab a shoe box or two to use to create separation in the drawers so you have a dedicated space for your tank tops, tee shirts, leggings, etc.
2. Empty the drawer onto a flat surface—your bed or the top of your dresser or even the floor.
3. Decide what you want to keep. Don't keep anything that you don't love or that doesn't spark joy. You know you love it if you get excited to wear it (and if you're bummed when it's dirty).
4. Fold the shirts you're keeping.
5. Starting with the darkest shirts, place shirts in the drawer vertically (like a file in a filing cabinet). Make sure you're folding the item to the height of the drawer so you're maximizing space and are not tempted to throw things on top.
6. Do the same for the pants you keep in drawers.
7. Lay matching socks on top of each other and fold them into thirds and stand them up in your sock drawer. (People usually ball them together and make that little potato thing; don't do that, it stretches out the elastic.)
8. Moving to your closet, make sure all the clothes and hangers are facing the same direction (which direction can be as polarizing as loading the toilet paper roll, so just pick a way that works for you).
9. Hang long, heavy, and dark clothes on the left.
10. Hang light, short, and white clothes on the right.

THE EXPERT:

Patty Morrissey is a lifestyle and organizing expert, and the founder of Clear & Cultivate, a therapeutic organizing and lifestyle company based in Huntington, New York. Patty was dubbed a "Magician" by *CBS This Morning* and "Guru of Tidiness" by the *New*

York Times. In 2016, she became one of the first certified KonMari Consultants outside of Japan and works closely with Marie Kondo as lead instructor of their consultant certification program.

THE EXPLANATION:

The key to clothing storage is visibility: Instead of stacking shirts on top of one another like you might see at the Gap, try the vertical file. It reduces wrinkles, since there isn't one stuck on the bottom, and you're not just grabbing the top two shirts over and over again. As you're folding, smooth out each item with your hand—the heat from your skin will flatten it out pretty effectively. This step also helps you notice imperfections, so if there's a stain or a hole or a button missing, don't put it back. For the closet, the key is to not cram so much in there that you can't slide the hangers around. Separating the long and short stuff creates space underneath the short clothes to store suitcases or boxes. And the color gradient makes good sense (where's my red shirt? oh, right!) and brings good vibes (research shows that seeing those color lines in our drawers and closets elicits positive feelings). There's also something really powerful about taking good care of things that no one else can see but you. You open your drawer or your closet, and there's a sense of peace and order like you have this under control. You want it to be set up like a boutique so it will be a joy to shop your closet.

Pro tip: Keep an "outbox" in your closet—any time you come across something you don't love, toss it in the outbox. Periodically empty it by donating the items or selling them on an app like Mercari or Poshmark.

A word from the fashion expert:

"Stop with the clothes that don't fit you anymore!" says Aya Kanai, editor in chief of *Marie Claire* (and former head of fashion for all Hearst publications). "Having pieces in your closet that make you feel guilty or bad about yourself in some way is not a good way to live. Our bodies change. Letting those items gather dust in your closet is not going to help you wear them at some future date. Somebody else should be enjoying those clothes!" The fashion resale market (i.e., buying secondhand clothes) has become so powerful and so important because the fashion industry is the second most-polluting industry in the world. Crazy, right? You can do your part by getting rid of the clothes that don't fit you anymore and letting someone else give them new life.

••• 6 •••

MAKE CHORES EASIER

WRITE A TO-DO LIST YOU'LL ACTUALLY CHECK OFF

1. Figure out your top 3–5 priorities (for work and life).
2. Write those priorities across the top of a big piece of paper, like column headers.
3. List your to-dos under the corresponding priority ("book massage" would go under "take better care of myself").
4. Notice there are tasks that don't align with any of your priorities (like calling the rental car company about that insane overcharge). Create an extra column called "the other 5 percent."
5. Mark like tasks with like tasks. Label the things that require focus "think work," while quick tasks can be broken into "5-minute action items" and "15-minute action items." (You can pick a color to represent each of these if that's your style.)
6. Think about the order in which you can best get these things done, and number them.
7. Transfer the to-dos into your calendar, scheduling a block of time for "think work," and smaller chunks for various "action items" you can group together.

THE EXPERT:

Christine Carter, Ph.D., is the author of *The Sweet Spot: How to Achieve More by Doing Less*. She's a sociologist and senior fellow at UC Berkeley's Greater Good Science Center.

THE EXPLANATION:

For a to-do list to be fulfilling (and successful), you need to feel like you're working toward the right things—so setting priorities is the first step. Those could range from "nurture my friendships" to "grow my business"; just keep it to five or fewer, as the brain gets overwhelmed if you try to focus on too many things at once. If you don't prioritize like this, it's possible to spend your whole day in "the other 5 percent" (you should spend no more than forty-five minutes on those annoying administrative tasks). It's also tremendously inefficient to go down every item on your to-do list one by one. Similar tasks should be done at the same time so you're not constantly interrupting your flow to flip-flop between things that require focus and things that are quick. Transferring the to-dos into your calendar is essential—if your brain doesn't know *when* it's going to do something it will continue to interrupt you (*OMG, I have to pick up dog food!*). And it doesn't work to just externalize that by writing it down; you have to know that you're picking up dog food on your way home from work on Tuesday. *Then* your brain will let it go.

Pro tip: Overwhelmed just looking at your list? You're doing something wrong. If you know you don't have time or just *won't* do something, *don't* put it on the list (that includes things you've been meaning to do since 2016, like make that $^!*@ photo album of your trip to Marbella). Sunday night is a great time to make a to-do list, then check and update it for a few minutes each day. If after five minutes you still find yourself color coding (hi!) and organizing, stop and get to work.

PAY YOUR BILLS

1. Set up electronic bill pay. This is a MUST for making things exponentially easier.
2. Determine what bill-paying schedule suits you. Ask yourself: "Will I pay bills as they come in? Will I set aside one day each week? Once a month?"
3. If you only want to deal with bills once a month, move your due dates to the *same date* for *every single bill*—otherwise, you'll end up with late fees.
4. Every time you sort your mail, put bills in the "to be dealt with" place. FOR HOW BEST TO OPEN MAIL, SEE PAGE 73.
5. When you set aside time to open your bills (daily, weekly, or monthly as determined in step 2), open all of them and pay all of them right then.
6. File or shred the bill.

THE EXPERT:

Corinne Morahan is the founder and CEO of Grid + Glam, a Boston-based full-service professional organizing company that marries aesthetics with functionality (her Instagram features drool-worthy desk and pantry makeovers). Corinne started her career working on Wall Street and leverages her financial experience in her current work.

THE EXPLANATION:

To make your bill-paying routine quick and simple, an up-front time investment is required but it will be well worth it. You'll need your bank account log-in information, copies of all your recurring bills, and about thirty to forty-five minutes. Log in and add each credit card or utility company as a "Payee." You'll be repeatedly asked if you'd like to eliminate paper bills and receive email statements and text alerts instead. This is tempting (and environmentally friendly) but unless you're *completely* on top of your email you should probably still get a paper bill. To get all your due dates synched up you'll need to do a bit of research to find out how each company handles it. Some allow you to do it online, directly in your account. Others require either a phone call or a written request for change. The one exception is subscription services (like Netflix) who bill you on the day you signed up and don't have the back-end flexibility to change the date. (The work-around there is to cancel your subscription and sign up again on the date you want to be billed.) And try to resist opening bills as you're walking back from your mailbox "just to see"—keep all the bills and any stress of opening said bills to one time and place. It will only take you minutes, you can do it from your phone, and you'll never need another stamp or check again.

Pro tip: If you aren't doing direct withdrawal, set a reminder on your phone or calendar to do the payment. And if you still forget and pay late, it's always worth calling and mentioning how much of a loyal client you are and asking them to reverse any fees and interest charges.

LOAD A DISHWASHER

1. Put all cups and glasses in the top rack—place tall glasses where they fit best without hitting spray arms, the door, or the top of the dishwasher (in some dishwashers the deeper areas are on the sides, in others they're in the middle). Leave a little room in between glasses.

2. Place small bowls and dishwasher-safe plastics in the top rack as well (scrape out any chunks of leftover food first). Cereal bowls should typically be loaded on the upper rack (check your manual to be sure) vertically between the tines that hold the dishes, but facing down and inward at a slightly acute angle

toward the bottom spray arm (don't place bowls completely flat upside down).

3. Load forks and spoons with the handles facing *down* to ensure the dirty parts of the utensils have contact with the water and detergent. (The basket would act as a barricade if the dirty parts were hidden inside it.)

4. Place knives blade end down so you don't cut yourself when it comes time to unload. (If your dishwasher has an open basket, mix spoons, forks, and knives to prevent them from nesting.)

5. Load the bottom rack starting with any large, caked-on dishes—place them facedown if nothing else is in the dishwasher or angled toward the lower spray arm if you're fitting other things around them. (Look for a dishwasher-safe indication on the bottom of any cookware you want to put in.)

6. Put oversize items, like platters and dishwasher-safe cutting boards, toward the sides and back so they don't block the water and detergent.

7. Fill in the bottom rack with plates (resting in the tines) and smaller dishes, making sure there is a little bit of space around each item. Resist the urge to overcrowd!

8. Put in a top-rated detergent and check that the rinse-aid dispenser is full (this enables faster, streak-free drying).

9. Before hitting start, run the kitchen sink tap until the water gets hot—otherwise the wash cycle will start with cold water, which is not how you want to wash your dishes.

THE EXPERT:

Consumer Reports is a pro-consumer advocacy nonprofit organization that helps people make informed decisions through research and testing. (They buy and test about thirty-five dishwashers a year, running almost two thousand different caked-on dishes and utensils through them to see what works best.)

THE EXPLANATION:

Loading the top rack first means you get the smaller stuff out of your sink and off your counters so you have more space to deal with the bigger, often dirtier dishes. If you prefer to load the bottom first you can, just fully load one rack before moving on to the next for maximum efficiency. You don't want to stick entire meals in the machine (we all know those people; I live with one), so scraping is good, but with today's dishwashers prerinsing really isn't necessary (we also know the people who basically wash their dishes before loading them; I am one). For the really caked-on stuff, you can soak in a soapy solution first. Some machines have special wash zones with turbo jets—read the manual for how to load those zones, since they vary from model to model. When loading, keep in mind there are usually two spray arms—one on the bottom and one attached to the upper rack. Some models even have a third attached to the top of the tub. Be sure things are aimed where they'll get cleanest and avoid overcrowding—when dishes are pressed up against each other it prevents the flow of water and detergent and can leave water spots at the contact points and cause breakages. And, let's be honest, in the time you'll spend rearranging the whole dishwasher to fit that one bowl, you could have hand-washed five of them. Remember, there's no trophy for fitting it all in. Wait, really?!

Bonus
......

Things you *shouldn't* put in your dishwasher: large kitchen knives (detergents can cause damage to the edges, and the heat can cause metal to soften), and anything made of brass, bronze, wood, and china with gold leaf. Pots and pans made of aluminum or stainless steel can usually go in the dishwasher, but nonstick pans, even if they say dishwasher safe, should be hand washed. Dishwasher-safe plastics always go on the top rack so they stay away from the heating element, which can cause warping.

Pro tip: Clean your dishwasher as needed by using a damp rag to wipe the seal between the dishwasher door and the tub, where residue and food particles collect. Buildup can cause odors, lead to mold growth, and potentially keep the door from sealing properly. Avoid bleach-based wipes, harsh chemicals, scouring pads, and anything abrasive on a stainless door and tub. If you live in an area with hard water, the inside of your dishwasher is likely to develop mineral films and discoloration (these deposits look like a cloudy film on your dishes and the interior of your machine). Use a citric acid–based dishwasher cleaner, such as Affresh or Finish, to remove the deposits monthly.

EMPTY A DISHWASHER

"Ask yourself what you're going to do with the next 4–6 minutes of your life. Is it really more important than having dishes? Because that's how long it will take to empty the dishwasher."
—Rachel Hoffman

Have a dish towel handy, and if something is wet, wipe it dry and put it away. (Don't create more work for yourself later by leaving it out to dry.)

1. Open the dishwasher and pull out the bottom rack.
2. Take out the silverware cage, put it next to the silverware drawer, and empty it.
3. Remove all the plates and stack them on the counter, then carry the stack to the cabinet.
4. Repeat for small plates and bowls.
5. Once the bottom is completely empty, slide it back in and pull out the top rack.
6. Take two glasses at a time from the dishwasher and put them away.

7. Put miscellaneous things—leftover containers, oversize dishes—in their home.

8. Oh, and you know that one stubborn fork or mug that you keep leaving in the dishwasher in hopes that *this* will be the time it finally gets clean? Grab it now, hand-wash it, dry it, and put it away.

THE EXPERT:

Rachel Hoffman is a cleaning expert and founder of Unfuck Your Habitat, a housekeeping and organizational system. She's the author of *Cleaning Sucks: An Unfuck Your Habitat Guided Journal for Less Mess, Less Stress, and a Home You Don't Hate.*

THE EXPLANATION:

People will put off emptying their dishwasher for *days*. But what would you be doing with those four to six minutes? Unless it's curing cancer, just make yourself empty the damn dishwasher. Do things in groupings—plates together, bowls together—because our brain likes order, and if you have a go-to system you'll eventually be able to go into autopilot on this. The reason you do the bottom rack first is that water often collects on the top of glasses or overturned bowls on the top rack, and if you slide that out first that dirty water sloshes down on the clean plates. Gross *and* inefficient. (You can also buy flat-bottom glasses to prevent the water from gathering there in the first place—noted!)

BUY ONLY WHAT YOU CAME FOR

1. Write a list of what you're going to the store to buy—even if it's just three things.

2. Stop at the ATM on the way there and take out the cash you need to buy *only* the thing(s) on your list. (Consult step 1 as needed.)

3. Leave your debit and credit cards inside the glove compartment of your car.

4. Go straight to the aisle where the thing(s) you need will be. (Ask customer service if you don't know and can't trust yourself to wander.)

5. If you spot something not on your list that you feel like you might buy, ask yourself four questions: "Do I need it? Do I love it? Do I like it? Do I want it?" (If it's a genuine need *or love*, fine; otherwise put it back and keep walking.)

6. Picture yourself when you're old and gray. Do you really want that version of you to be struggling financially because present you couldn't stop buying faux-fur pillows at Target?

THE EXPERT:

Tiffany Aliche, aka "the Budgetnista," is a financial educator and author of *The One Week Budget* and *Live Richer Challenge*. In 2019 she wrote and helped pass "the Budgetnista Law," which makes it mandatory for financial education to be integrated into all middle schools in New Jersey. She created Live Richer Academy, which teaches women how to create, implement, and automate their own personalized financial freedom plan.

THE EXPLANATION:

You need a game plan or you're doomed. Can you just do a walk of shame back to your car for the credit cards? Yes. And you might. But having to make that extra effort gives you pause about the purchases. As does the priority check: Is this a need, is this a love, is this a like, or is it a want? (Tiffany wears bracelets with those four questions on them.) We all have to spend on needs—food, shelter, medication, transportation—but we typically skip over the love because those things take more patience and time to pay for. So we spend on *likes* or *wants*. When you're younger, it's hard to care too much about your older self, so make her a caricature. Tiffany's eighty-year-old self is named Wanda, and she's sassy and always minding everyone's business. Think of them like a grandparent. Would you ever ask Grandma to work so you can chill and over-spend in your thirties or forties? Bottom line: If you're not smart about your money now, Wanda's gonna pay for it later.

Pro tip: Get a small address label and write, "need it, love it, like it, want it." Adhere it to the same place where the activation sticker used to be. Every time you pull out that card, you'll be reminded to check your priorities. (This is especially handy if you prefer to use a particular card for the perks instead of using cash or if you, ahem, have a Target card.)

Bonus

Create a "say yes" plan. Identify something you love and want to work toward buying (plane tickets to Paris, for example). Next time you say no to yourself for something you don't really need, reframe it—instead of saying no to takeout for dinner again you're saying yes to Paris. This is a great way to make yourself feel less deprived when you skip the "likes and wants" purchases; you'll feel invigo-rated because it reminds you of that bigger and better thing you're saving for. (It works on friends, too—"*Sorry, girls, I have to say no to brunch this weekend because I'm saying yes to Paris.*") Tiffany's trick for figuring out what a love is: Ask yourself if you had Oprah's bank account, what would you do . . . or do more of? Travel? Start a busi-ness? Spend time with family and friends? Go see a play? These are the purchases that make life full and fun. If you focus on needs and loves in lieu of likes and wants, you've chosen to use your money to live purposefully and passionately.

MAKE A GROCERY LIST

1. Take out your calendar and see what the week has in store (how many nights will you be cooking, are you packing lunches, any special activities or friends coming over on the weekend?).
2. Plan what meals you can, and write down those ingredients.
3. Check your refrigerator and pantry to see what staples you're low on (eggs, greens, coffee, that really good truffle cheese from Trader Joe's), and add those to the list.
4. Shop your backstock. Go to wherever you keep your extra food (the garage? the basement? that corner cabinet that's really hard to open?) and see if you actually *have* any of the things on your list. If you do, cross them off (*that* feels good).
5. Scan your list and try to get it organized by sections of the store—rearrange if you think it will help.
6. Take the reusable grocery bags out to your car now so you don't forget them when you go. Or keep them in the trunk.

THE EXPERT:

Michele Vig is the founder and chief organizer at Neat Little Nest, a Minneapolis-based home organization company.

THE EXPLANATION:

Knowing how much food you need (or don't need) for the week is the most important step to prevent overshopping. This will help you control your budget and your waste—throwing out food that sat untouched until it wilted or expired is just depressing. Part of adulting is being a little more thoughtful about what's coming up so you're not scrambling in the moment. If it's more likely you'll be picking up a rotisserie chicken on the way home than actually cooking one, don't put "chicken" on the list. (And save yourself the guilt—we all take shortcuts.) Friends coming over Saturday? Shop for snacks *now*. Make sure that your household favorites are either *in* the house or on the list. And if you organize the list in a way that groups like things together, you'll be able to buzz down the aisles.

Pro tip: An organized pantry and refrigerator makes grocery shopping so much easier. Michele recommends "decanting"— taking food out of plastic and cardboard packaging and storing it in glass jars or clear plastic containers. Food stays fresher and it's more pleasing to the eye, sure, but it also saves you time and frustration. Having, say, granola bars in a basket and cereal in a glass container makes inventory checks easier because you can quickly see exactly how much of something you have left—no need to shake the box. And when your pantry looks nice and organized—and isn't full of the word pollution and overstimulation of modern food packaging—it brings you an unexpected hit of joy and peace in a place that was typically unjoyful, which makes mealtime and putting away the groceries just a little bit more fun. Yes, please!

BAG YOUR GROCERIES

1. While shopping, pack your cart with the heavy items toward the front—or on the bottom level where you can grab them easily (keep light produce and easily damaged goods in the basket, unless there's a kid in there).
2. When loading the conveyer belt sort your items by weight, placing heavier items on the conveyor belt *first*, then boxed goods.
3. Put your herbs, chips, and light items on the belt *last*.
4. Use reusable bags—good for the environment, yes, but also good for the bagger, since they won't rip and they hold more.
5. Treat each bag like you're building a house. Start by putting up the walls, which are your boxed goods (cereal, tissues, granola bars). Place them around the edges of the bag.

6. Put canned items, jars, and other heavy things neatly in the middle of the bag; those are your "furniture." (Don't let glass touch glass.)

7. Lay your produce, chips, and other light stuff on top of the heavy stuff—these are your "decorations," and they go *upstairs* in the house.

8. Keep frozen items together so they stay cold (and so you know which bag to unpack first when you get home).

9. Always put eggs and bread right on top of one of your bags.

10. Bag raw meat separately (you may also want to separate any chemicals or cleaning products). It's best to use a plastic bag for the meats in case any juices leak (you don't want that mess in your reusable bags—or your car). The good news: Many grocery stores now use compostable plastic bags for this step.

11. If there happens to be a person there to bag your groceries, let them.

THE EXPERT:

Dwayne Campbell is a veteran Hy-Vee supermarket chain employee who won the 2019 National Championship as the country's Best Bagger at the National Grocers Association competition (he was judged on speed, proper bag-building technique, and weight distribution, in addition to attitude and style). Hy-Vee is an employee-owned corporation operating more than 265 retail stores across eight Midwestern states.

THE EXPLANATION:

The key to easy and efficient bagging is sending things down the conveyer belt in the right order, which may mean rethinking how you pack your cart. If all the light stuff is on top it'll wind up going in the bags first (or crowding the bagging area), which is not what you want. Being just a little bit mindful of how you place your groceries makes it so much easier for the bagger (or you) to stack them properly. Putting up "walls" on the edges of the bags will keep jars of tomato sauce, bags of apples or potatoes, and bottles upright, so the bag doesn't become unwieldy (it'll also prevent cans from punching through the bag). Ideally, you want each bag to weigh about the same to make carrying them more manageable, so keep an eye on overstuffing. And save chips for the very end. They're the hardest to bag because they take up so much space, and you can't maneuver around them because of all the air. When you "build a house" with a plastic bag, you have to be a bit more diligent with it because corners of boxes can poke through the sides. Pack carefully and make those houses a little smaller, putting fewer items in each bag—at Hy-Vee they have a saying: "Eight is great."

Pro tip: Put all your pantry items together in one (or two) bags so when you get home you just take that bag to the pantry and unload all at once.

WASH A LOAD OF LAUNDRY

1. Choose *one* load to tackle every day (darks, whites, or delicates, for example; or choose a family member's laundry for each day).
2. Unball the socks, inside out the pants, spray any stains (SEE PAGE 93 FOR HOW TO TREAT TRICKY STAINS) and put it all in the machine.
3. Use your hand to make sure you can still move clothes around freely in the machine (i.e., don't overstuff it).
4. Add the detergent to the dispenser and adjust your settings accordingly (in general, darks are washed on cold, whites on warm or hot, and delicates on delicate or the "hand wash" setting). Note: Sometimes powdered laundry soap dissolves better in a front loader when put directly in the drum.
5. If you think you'll forget that you just put a load in (hi!), set a timer on your phone.

6. Once the wash cycle is over, shake everything out and put it in the dryer (removing anything you want to air-dry, like those new jeans that are a leeeetle hard to put on).

7. Scrape the lint off the vent, close the dryer, and start the cycle.

8. When the dryer dings, take the laundry directly to where you like to fold (bedrooms are the most common) and PUT. IT. AWAY.

THE EXPERT:

Becky Rapinchuk, aka "Clean Mama," is a cleaning and home organization expert and the author of three books, including *Simply Clean: The Proven Method for Keeping Your Home Organized, Clean, and Beautiful in Just 10 Minutes a Day* and *Clean Mama's Guide to a Healthy Home*. She also has a Clean Mama product line.

THE EXPLANATION:

Doing a daily load of laundry from start to finish (washed, dried, folded, and *put away*) probably sounds daunting, but a little bit every day is easier than *all* the bits on one day—and, bonus, you'll always have clean clothes! Throw it in first thing in the a.m. or load the washer at night and set it to run in the morning an hour before you wake up. Don't have enough for a load a day? Try every other day. And if you never seem to have enough for a full white load, you can really wash most things together on cold (particularly kids' clothes, which Becky suggests doing by *kid* rather than color—that way each child's clothes stay together throughout the process and you cut out that sorting step). Getting the clothes right side outed—if that's not the technical term, it should be—at this stage saves time when you're folding and putting away, which is by far the more annoying task.

Bonus

Safer alternatives you can DIY. Most fabric softeners and dryer sheets contain artificial fragrances and toxic ingredients (and coat clothing fibers which makes them harder to get clean over time). Instead, try a quarter cup of white vinegar in the wash (put it in the fabric softener slot—you won't smell like salad dressing, promise!) and use wool dryer balls. Wool is biodegradable and naturally antimicrobial—toss three in the dryer with each load to soften clothes and reduce drying time (they're reusable and last up to one thousand uses). If you think you'll miss that clean laundry smell, put a couple drops of essential oil on each ball.

REMOVE A STAIN

1. Working over a sink or wash basin, apply a stain solution to the stain.
2. Gently work the solution into the stained area with a clean, soft bristled brush (or your finger).
3. Pour hot water from a height onto the stain (it's more effective that way). If it's blood, put the item right under the faucet—the pressure will help work the stain—and use *cool* water. Do not use hot water on silk, wool, or cashmere—use cold water only for these fabrics.
4. Allow the item to soak in a bath of warm water (for bloodstains and delicate fabrics like silk and cashmere, use cool water and don't soak silk longer than 30 minutes at a time).
5. If the stain has faded but isn't completely gone, repeat the process until satisfied.
6. Launder the garment as normal. (For garments made of silk, wool, or cashmere, hand-wash in cool water.)
7. To treat stubborn stains, you can create a paste with a stain solution and an all-purpose bleach alternative. Work the paste into the stained area with a brush and follow steps 3–5. Do not use bleach alternative on silk, wool, or cashmere.

8. Make sure you remove all stains before putting clothes in the dryer. Items made of silk, wool, and cashmere need to be air-dried.

9. Do not iron stained items.

THE EXPERTS:

Gwen Whiting and Lindsey Boyd, cofounders of the Laundress, a premium global brand with an eco-friendly collection of detergent, fabric care, and home cleaning products. The Laundress's mission is to turn necessary domestic chores into a luxurious experience by pairing effective products with the know-all to clean with confidence.

THE EXPLANATION:

For optimal stain removal, you should reference the specific fabric and stain you're treating to determine the appropriate product, water temperature, and technique to use. (On the Laundress site, they have a fill-in-the blanks stain guide where you can get exact instructions for your particular stain and garment.) You want a stain solution that can target and break down stubborn stains like red wine, sauce, chocolate, grass, coffee/tea, and pit stains. Pouring water on the stain and then soaking is an important step but needs to be tweaked based on the stain and fabric (blood, for example, requires cold water, as hot water can cause the stain to set in).

Bonus

For oil-based stains, you can use a stain bar. (The Laundress makes a Wash & Stain Bar for this purpose.) Or try this hack from "Clean Mama" Becky Rapinchuk: Keep a piece of white chalk in the laundry room to rub on grease stains and absorb the oil (it should also do the trick on butter, salad dressing, cooking oil, etc.). Launder as usual, and the piece should come out clean!

KEEP TOWELS FRESH, SOFT, AND SMELLING GOOD

1. Make sure your towel storage method is optimal for nonstinky towels (if my 12-year-old son is reading this, "rolled in a ball on your bedroom floor" is not optimal). Keep them stored somewhere clean and dry.

2. Hang postshower towels so they're able to fully dry in between uses. (If your bathroom is particularly steamy and doesn't have a fan, consider hanging the towels in your bedroom until they're dry.)

3. Use bath towels no more than twice before washing.

4. Don't toss wet towels in a hamper or laundry basket—hang them to dry first, *then* move them to the dirty laundry.

5. Change your hand towels often (daily is optimal).

6. Never leave towels (or any laundry, for that matter) longer than a couple hours in the washing machine. The wet towels and closed space are breeding grounds for bacteria and smells to build up.

7. Don't overfill your washing machine or dryer; you want adequate water flow in the wash and adequate airflow in the dryer to clean and dry your towels (and any laundry).

8. If you have extra-stinky towels, put them in a wash cycle using ½ cup baking soda (put it right in the drum, not the dispenser) and warm water; then rewash them with your regular detergent.

9. Stop using fabric softener—it coats the fibers and can keep your towels from getting fully clean and fluffy (not to mention it's full of potentially harmful chemicals that you don't need in your home). SEE PAGE 92 FOR A DIY ALTERNATIVE.

10. Fold towels as soon as they come out of the dryer.

11. Clean your washing machine regularly (read the manual for the best way to do this).

THE EXPERT:

Becky Rapinchuk, aka "Clean Mama," is a cleaning and home organization expert and the author of three books, including *Simply Clean: The Proven Method for Keeping Your Home Organized, Clean, and Beautiful in Just 10 Minutes a Day* and *Clean Mama's Guide to a Healthy Home*. She also has a Clean Mama product line.

THE EXPLANATION:

Towels absorb water (that is, after all, their purpose) and if they aren't hung up properly that water will remain there for too long and become a breeding ground for bacteria. Then they get stinky (and harder to unstink). Overstuffing is a problem, too—in the hamper, in the washing machine, in the dryer. Think of giving your towels room to breathe. And as soon as they're out of the dryer, fold them (and—bonus points—*put them away*) to prevent them from getting wrinkled and crunchy.

Bonus

One easy way to simplify your laundry: Switch to all white towels (and sheets while you're at it). Why? You can wash the towels all at once, and they can be washed on hot or sanitized when needed without fading. You can also launder them with bleach alternative to remove stains or dinginess. And white towels add a spa-like look to your bathrooms—and match with just about any color or decor.

Pro tip: Got a smelly tee that isn't getting unsmelly? Put it in a ziplock bag and put in the freezer overnight—this will kill bacteria, which is what makes fabric smell.

FOLD A FITTED SHEET

1. Place your sheet on a flat surface with the fitted corners facing up.
2. Square up and smooth out all corners and elastic as much as you can.
3. Fold the sheet in half horizontally, taking care to keep the fitted part tucked under and even. Smooth it out so the folds are lined up on top of each other and nothing is bunched underneath.
4. Tuck the top fitted corners into the bottom fitted corners.
5. Fold the sheet horizontally again so all four corners are stacked.
6. Smooth out with your hands.
7. Place the top set of corners into the bottom set again.
8. Fold the sheet in half the other way and in half again (repeat the folding as many times as you'd like).

Step 1

Step 2

Step 3

Step 4

Step 5

Step 6

THE EXPERT:

Ariel Kaye is the founder and CEO of Parachute, a modern lifestyle brand, and author of *How to Make a House a Home: Creating a Purposeful, Personal Space.* She first launched Parachute as an online-only brand with a curated assortment of bedding products (it was named after the way the fabric billows when you shake out your sheets!). Parachute has since opened brick-and-mortar stores across the country and expanded to include bath, furniture, tabletop, and a baby collection.

THE EXPLANATION:

The struggle is real, but it doesn't have to be! The fitted sheet is famously difficult to fold, but if you take it step by step you can save time and sanity (and space in your linen closet). Smoothing each layer as you go is key to keeping the whole package from getting too puffy. A slightly less adult hack (and my personal workaround until writing this book): Only own one set of sheets so you wash and put them back on in the same day, never having to fold anything!

IRON A SHIRT

1. Read the tag to see which setting to use and adjust the iron accordingly.
2. Pop the collar and iron the inside, then flip and do the outside, pressing from the tips toward the middle. (Keep the collar up until the rest of the shirt is ironed.)
3. Iron each cuff (make sure they're unbuttoned) horizontally with the tip of the iron pointed toward the sleeve, starting on the inside; then flip the cuff to repeat on the outside.
4. Lay a sleeve on the board, back side facing up, and smooth front and back layers flat (double-check for any creases before applying the iron). In long strokes, iron a straight crease at the top of the arm. Flip and do the front side, then repeat on the other arm.
5. Slide the open sleeve over the tip of the board and iron each shoulder flat.
6. Lay the open shirt facedown and hit the yoke. (What's the yoke, you ask? It's that double-layer strip along the back that connects the collar to the body.) Swing the iron from shoulder

to midback on each side. Then finish the back, ironing below the yoke from top to bottom.

7. Iron the front, beginning on the nonbutton side. Start on the strip with the buttonholes (fun fact: it's called the placket) and work outward, using long strokes, from the collar down. If there's a pocket, press it from the bottom up.

8. Finish with the front-button side, weaving the iron in and around the buttons.

9. Hang your shirt up immediately so you don't have to do this all over again.

THE EXPERTS:

Gwen Whiting and Lindsey Boyd are the cofounders of the Laundress, an ecofriendly line of detergent and fabric care sold around the world (even in Estonia!).

THE EXPLANATION:

Always read the label first, but don't be deterred if it says "dry-clean only" (90 percent of dry-clean-only garments can be washed and

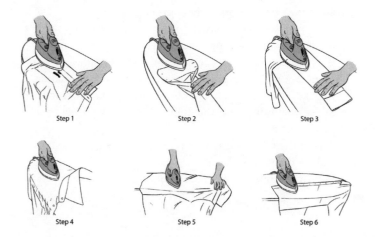

Step 1   Step 2   Step 3

Step 4   Step 5   Step 6

ironed at home). Cottons and linens are always safe to iron; if your shirt is synthetic, test a small area first. (And never iron wool, velvet, or corduroy—ironing will crush or flatten the natural pile.) The collar has to come first because if you save it till last, you'll wrinkle the whole shirt and have to double your efforts (d'oh!). When it comes to the arms, hold up a sleeve and tug taut along the seam so you've got a crisp, straight fold from shoulder to cuff before laying it down; this prevents pressing in any unwanted lines. Hitting the front sleeves and body last means you can easily correct mistakes in the areas where you want your best work (i.e., the part you see in the mirror and people see coming at them).

PUT ON A DUVET COVER

1. Lay the duvet insert flat on top of the bed.
2. Turn your duvet cover inside out.
3. Grab the two top corners of your duvet cover.
4. With your hands inside each corner of the duvet cover, grab the top two corners of your duvet insert.
5. Use the ties to secure the duvet insert to the duvet by tying them around the corner of the duvet insert you're holding.
6. Flip the duvet cover right side out, enveloping the insert as you go.
7. Shake and fluff so that the duvet cover is completely covering your insert.
8. Secure the ties in the last two corners.
9. Button the buttons.
10. Give it one more shake, then smooth out across your bed.

THE EXPERT:

Ariel Kaye is the founder and CEO of Parachute, a modern lifestyle brand, and author of *How to Make a House a Home: Creating a Purposeful, Personal Space.* She first launched Parachute as an online-only brand with a curated assortment of bedding products (it was named after the way the fabric billows when you shake out your sheets!). Parachute has since opened brick-and-mortar stores across the country and expanded to include bath, furniture, tabletop, and a baby collection.

THE EXPLANATION:

Almost as bad as folding a fitted sheet is putting on a #$@% duvet cover. But it's important. Did you know that 40 percent of Americans don't use a top sheet, they just sleep between a fitted sheet and a duvet comforter? Same goes for most of Europe. The top sheet is a personal option—there for the taking, but only if you want it (Parachute sells their top sheets separately). Some people find it more natural and less constricting, and the duvet cover just gets tossed in the wash with the sheets. And yes, that makes regularly washing your duvet cover all the more important, since the oils from your skin are directly touching the cover. Oh, and SEE PAGE 4 FOR HOW TO MAKE YOUR BED!

··· 7 ···

CLEAN ANYTHING

TIDY A ROOM IN TEN MINUTES OR LESS

1. Grab some paper towels or a rag and a cleaning spray to take with you to the room you'll be tidying.
2. Set a timer for 10 minutes.
3. Look for things that have the potential to smell—dirty dishes, garbage, laundry—and move them to where they really belong.
4. Scan flat surfaces and either put the stuff on them away or make piles.
5. Use the paper towels or rag to wipe down the exposed flat surfaces.
6. Leave the room for a beat, come back in, and see what catches your eye (in a bad way), then address that.

THE EXPERT:

Rachel Hoffman is the founder of Unfuck Your Habitat, a housekeeping and organizational system. She's the author of *Unfuck Your Habitat: You're Better Than Your Mess* and *Cleaning Sucks: An Unfuck Your Habitat Guided Journal for Less Mess, Less Stress, and a Home You Don't Hate.*

THE EXPLANATION:

Setting a timer keeps you from being overwhelmed by the enormity of the task and reframes tidying up as something you can do in little blips of time (i.e., you don't have to let things go until you've got time for a marathon session). No matter what room you're working on, always deal with the stuff that could wind up stinking first, then the flat surfaces—tabletops, dressers, counters. They accumulate the most stuff, and making them tidy immediately makes the whole room feel neater. Leaving quickly and reentering will help you figure out what might be subconsciously ticking you off so you can remove that—those are often the roadblocks to tidiness in the first place. Even in ten minutes you'll be able to see a visible difference, which means you'll be more willing to keep things neat (and to invest another ten when you've got 'em).

Bonus

Here's a mantra for when you walk in your door: "Don't put it down, put it away." Your shoes, for example. How much more time does it take to put them in the closet instead of just kicking them off on the floor? Less than thirty seconds. But a week later when you have seven pairs of shoes by the door that need to be dealt with, it's a bigger task (and one you're more likely to avoid). And since it's easier to "put it away" when everything has a place to go, create a home for every item with tools like shelves, baskets, hangers, and hooks (got kids? put some hooks at their height and teach them to hang their own stuff!).

CLEAN YOUR FLOORS

"You can get away with cleaning less when you clean more often."
—Donna Smallin Kuper

1. Pick everything up off the floor (shoes, toys, books, etc.).
2. Roll up any small throw rugs. There will be dirt *in* them and *under* them—take outside and shake them out.

3. Vacuum loose debris off hard floors or use a broom to sweep all the debris together then vacuum that up.
4. While you have your vacuum out, use the brush attachment to dust windowsills, lamp shades, and baseboards.
5. For mopping hard woods, use water only. (I know!)
6. Mop your way out the door of each room by starting at the farthest point away and working your way back. Don't walk on the floor while it's wet. You may see footprints, especially if you're barefoot.
7. Clean your cleaning tools when you're finished (remove hair and lint from your broom, empty the vacuum canister, clip any long hairs or threads from the brush roller).

THE EXPERT:

Donna Smallin Kuper is a certified house cleaning technician, organizing expert, and author of *Cleaning Plain & Simple*.

THE EXPLANATION:

You want to remove as much debris as possible before mopping; otherwise you're just pushing dirt around. And, yes, all you need on hardwood floors is water. So freeing, right?! And good for the environment. Water is what the manufacturers recommend, and some can void your warranty if you use anything other than that. (Spot clean areas that need extra TLC.) Buy a mop and get two microfiber mop heads so you always have a clean head ready to go. Just spritz with water.

Bonus

Always dust before you vacuum. The reason: gravity. This is also why you should dust from the top down. You'll need a microfiber cloth and water—keep it in a spray bottle so it's at the ready and so you're not running the cloth under the faucet to get it damp (it will get too wet to work properly). Remember that you're *collecting* the dust, not brushing it off. Go slowly and deliberately. And don't forget the most forgotten areas—the blades of a ceiling fan can get really nasty, especially in a kitchen. Baseboards, too, can get built up with grime, and once that happens you can't just dust them anymore. Incorporate these areas into your cleaning routine to prevent them from becoming a more difficult job.

A word about routine:

You should have one! The more routine you are about cleaning, the easier and faster it will go. It's good to go in the same order—whatever way works for you, but do it the same way every time—so you really get it down pat, and the whole thing becomes more efficient. Also, your floors will stay cleaner if you do a quick sweep daily. As Donna says, "*When it comes to cleaning, it's a lot easier to keep up than it is to catch up.*"

A word about microfiber:

Microfiber cloths are made of very small (hence the name) synthetic fibers that capture dirt, dust, and even bacteria. They're super absorbent and dry quickly, and they can be used for cleaning almost any surface with nothing more than a little water. To care for them, wash cloths together (with no other clothes or towels) in hot water with a little detergent and no fabric softener, and dry them on low heat or hang to dry. They should last for fifty washings. (If you don't care for them properly, the little tentacles get clogged and they don't work well.)

Pro tip: When vacuuming carpets, pushing the vacuum forward is called the positioning pass (it's mostly about getting the vacuum into the right position) and when you pull it back *that's* the working pass. It's the pulling motion that actually removes soil, so go slow.

CLEAN THE KITCHEN AFTER DINNER

"Get yourself to 'sink zero' before bed. This is the reset. If you leave stuff soaking for tomorrow, you're compounding your work. Do future you a favor and set yourself up for a better morning."

—Rachel Hoffman

1. Clear one countertop to use as your staging ground for the dirty dishes. (If you cleaned as you cooked—which, yeah, you should try to do—this may already be done.)
2. Stash pots and pans and big stuff someplace where they're accessible but not in the way (on the stove is a good spot). If any have to soak, fill them with warm, soapy water and let them sit on the stove while you go through the next steps.
3. Pack up any leftovers—SEE PAGE 141—and put away the other things that came out of the fridge or pantry (give them a wipe-down with a damp cloth or wet paper towel if needed; looking at you, ketchup bottle).
4. Empty out the sink, putting things in the dishwasher or hand-washing them and setting them out to dry.
5. a) If you're someone who needs to see the whole job in front of you, bring everything off the table and lay it all on that clean counter.

   b) If you're someone who gets easily overwhelmed and is less likely to finish the job if it looks too daunting, clear in *stages*—all the silverware first, then the plates, then the cups, or one whole place setting at a time, and deal with each group before going back to the table for more.
6. Scrape, rinse, and load everything into the dishwasher that will fit. FOR THE BEST WAY TO LOAD SEE PAGE 81.
7. Wash the pots and bigger pans, one at a time, in the sink.
8. Wipe down all your countertops and the kitchen table.

9. Clean off any appliances that got splattered, wipe the handles of the refrigerator, and sweep the floors and/or pick up chicken nuggets that might have been flung from the table.

THE EXPERT:

Rachel Hoffman is a cleaning expert and founder of Unfuck Your Habitat, a housekeeping and organizational system. She's the author of *Cleaning Sucks: An Unfuck Your Habitat Guided Journal for Less Mess, Less Stress, and a Home You Don't Hate.*

THE EXPLANATION:

When it comes to cleaning you always want to make space for what you have to do, so clearing one counter is key—plus, seeing that surface will motivate you to keep going (cleanliness begets cleanliness). Avoid clearing dirty dishes and pans into the sink, because it makes the sink unusable—it's difficult/frustrating to rinse dishes when pots and pans are sloshing around in there. How you clear the table is based on personal preference. Just beware of stacking food-filled plates on top of each other; the potatoes from the top of one plate get mashed onto the bottom of another, and you've just doubled your work. And here's the thing about soaking dishes—it's a form of procrastination. They may need soaking, sure, but you know you're going to leave them in the sink, aren't you? Avoid that by not putting them there in the first place (there's no law that says you have to soak stuff in the sink). At the end of the day you want to reset everything back to clean. Don't make future you pay for present you's laziness. So dry the pots and put them away before you consider the kitchen closed. Serious bonus points if the dishwasher is finished running and you empty it before shutting down for the night. FOR HOW TO DO THAT SEE PAGE 84.

A word about cleaning and kids:

Kids are always listening so make sure you're not making chores such a chore—if you're cleaning the kitchen, don't complain about how awful it is. You don't have to have a dance party every time you're filling the dishwasher, but think about what kind of message it sends to them if you're always complaining about this stuff. You want to model a good attitude when it comes to housework. No, it's not super fun but it's just what we do, part of our everyday life like brushing our teeth. And think twice before using cleaning or chores as punishment: It can create trauma-based aversions to cleaning down the road!

CLEAN A SHOWER AND/OR TUB

1. Remove everything from the shower: bottles, soaps, sponges.
2. Pull the curtains out of the way—flip them up over the shower bar or remove them altogether.
3. Spray your cleaner liberally all over the shower walls but not the tub or floor yet.
4. Wait 5 minutes to let the product work.
5. Using the scrubby side of a two-sided sponge, work section by section on the shower walls—start at the top and work your way down in an S pattern. Keep doing this until all walls have been cleaned. Do not rinse.
6. Repeat steps 3, 4, and 5 for the tub. (Warning! If your tub is acrylic, use the soft side of your sponge only—the scrubbing side can ruin the finish.) The tub comes second in the event you need to step into it to get to the tiles. If you don't need to step into the shower to do this, feel free to do tub and tiles together.
7. Crank the shower on hot, and with a removable shower head spray the walls, following the same pattern you used to clean it. If you don't have a removable head, fill a jug to rinse the walls.

8. Use your microfiber cloth (or a squeegee if you have one handy) and wipe down the walls until the shower is dry and sparkling. Repeat for the tub. Don't forget to shine the chrome!

THE EXPERT:

Melissa Maker is the host of the CleanMySpace YouTube channel (she has more than 1.3 million subscribers) and the founder of Clean My Space, a housekeeping service based in her native Canada. She's the author of *Clean My Space: The Secret to Cleaning Better, Faster—and Loving Your Home Every Day.*

THE EXPLANATION:

When it comes to cleaning the shower walls, you really have to stick to the S pattern and avoid the temptation to scrub in circles—a total time waster. The key is getting the soap scum off, which is why using a good product is so important as is giving it "dwell time" to work. The longer you let it sit, the more it will break down the scum, the easier your job will be. Don't worry about spraying any higher than the tallest person that uses that shower, since you won't get any soap scum up there. And if you have glass shower walls, put full-strength vinegar in a spray bottle and just spritz that right on as your cleaner. When it comes time to clean the tub, roll up a towel to kneel on and don't forget to clean the inside of the tub wall you're leaning on—that's often forgotten.

Bonus

Clean all flat surfaces using Melissa's S pattern. Start at the top left-hand corner of the designated area and, applying constant pressure, work your way over to the top right-hand corner and then shift down and move back to the left, zigzagging your way to the bottom. It's one of the most efficient methods of cleaning and should replace the circle method most of us rock (think about it:

When you clean in a circle, you're bringing dirt from the uncleaned area right into the area you just cleaned).

Pro tip: Most people don't realize how powerful cleaning products are but *only* if they're used correctly—a lot of us don't do that, so we question their efficacy. They need to be liberally applied and they need time to work, about three to five minutes to penetrate the dirt and grime on a surface.

CLEAN A TOILET (IN THREE MINUTES!)

"Don't be afraid of work like this, it keeps you humble and reminds you to appreciate a clean space."

—Melissa Maker

1. Spray the whole thing from top to bottom with an all-purpose cleaner. (Spray the base and the floor around the toilet, too, especially if you have males in your house—guys, you know what you've done.)
2. Add the toilet bowl cleaner into the bowl and let it soak for a few minutes.
3. In order, wipe the tank lid, the flusher, and the tank itself down using a paper towel in an S pattern, then toss the paper towel.
4. Clean the top of the lid, then flip it up and clean under the lid.
5. Crumple up that paper towel so you get some hard edges and get into the area around the hinges, then toss that paper towel.
6. With a new paper towel, wipe the top of the seat, then the bottom, and leave the seat up (and toss that paper towel).
7. With a new paper towel, clean the area at the top of the bowl, then go all the way down the exterior of the bowl, the base of the toilet, and the area on the floor around the toilet.

8. Using a toilet brush, scrub under the rim (not too vigorously, or you'll get backsplash) and work your way around. Then, spiral the brush around the inside of the bowl, starting at the top and swirling it around until it gets to the chute. Pump the brush into the chute a few times.
9. Flush, rinsing the brush in the clean water.
10. Hold the brush at the edge of the bowl and flip the seat down so it traps the handle with the head hanging over the water. Leave it there to drip-dry.

THE EXPERT:

Melissa Maker is the host of the CleanMySpace YouTube channel (she has more than 1.3 million subscribers) and the founder of Clean My Space, a housekeeping service based in her native Canada. She's the author of *Clean My Space: The Secret to Cleaning Better, Faster—and Loving Your Home Every Day.*

THE EXPLANATION:

Remember to spray your product liberally so it can do the work for you. You'll notice toilet bowl cleaners have an angled spout—that's so you can get it under the rim easily (slowly glide the nozzle around the inner rim of the bowl, squeezing out the product in a steady, even flow).

When it comes to cleaning a toilet, paper towels are better than washable cloths because, well, toilets (you may also want to wear rubber gloves, your call). Work from top to bottom, and change the paper towel as it becomes too saturated (typically you'll need four per toilet). Toss them in the bathroom trash can then empty it when you're finished. The last step is key so you don't have to deal with a drippy toilet brush or store it wet, which can lead to yuck. You can clean the brush occasionally by soaking it in a bucket filled with a solution of one scoop oxygen bleach powder mixed with hot water. Leave for thirty minutes, rinse well, and allow to drip-dry over the bucket.

8

BE HANDY

HANG A PICTURE

1. Look at the back of your frame to see if it has hardware attached for hanging (most do, or at least include it along with instructions for how to assemble).

2. If there's no hardware, buy picture-hanging wire from the hardware store and install on the back of the frame.

3. Measure the height and width of the frame (use a measuring tape), then place painter's tape in those dimensions on the wall where you want your picture to go.

4. Step back and walk by a few times to make sure you like where you're planning to put the picture. Artwork should be at eye level for *most* people (many people hang it too high).

5. When hanging pictures over a standard couch, you want art to go 6–8 inches above the highest cushion. Be sure the art will feel like a part of the surrounding furniture or objects, not floating separately above them.

6. Determine your mode of hanging by the weight of your art. Use a photo hanger for medium items up to 35 pounds—these are little V-shaped tools you can pick up at the hardware store; smaller items can just hang on a nail or a screw; and anything

above 35 pounds needs an anchor (and may be better hung by a professional).

7. Use a measuring tape to determine how far down the hanger is from the top of the frame.

8. Mark that spot on the wall by measuring the distance you got in step 7 from the top of the painter's tape.

9. Screw or nail your chosen mode of hardware into the wall.

10. Hang your photo.

11. If you have a level, use it to make sure the picture is straight. Otherwise, take a big step back and get it as level as possible by eyeballing it.

12. Apply earthquake putty to the inside bottom corners of the frame to make sure they stay in place (you can find this in the hardware store, in the photo-hanging section).

13. Once you've mastered this skill, don't tell your friends—they'll call you every time they have something to hang!

THE EXPERT:

Jasmine Roth is the host of HGTV's *Hidden Potential* and the winner of HGTV's *Rock the Block*. On *Hidden Potential*, she transforms builder-basic houses into custom dream homes. She also founded and runs Built Custom Homes, which manages the design of ground-up residential new-construction projects in Huntington Beach, California.

THE EXPLANATION:

The old adage—measure twice, cut once—applies here as well. The more you prepare, the easier this is going to be. Take your time, measure it all out, think through the placement, and *then* start putting holes in the wall. (But if you mess up it's OK. SEE PAGE 115 FOR HOW TO PATCH A HOLE IN YOUR WALL.) Step 3 is key, as it allows you to map out where you want the art to go. If you don't have a measuring tape—though Jasmine believes, and I concur, that *every* home should have one—you can use a string or a shoelace to measure. Picture hanging wire is a great hack because you can still adjust and straighten the photo once it's up (i.e., you don't have to be on-the-money level). Even better: earthquake putty (Jasmine discovered this when she moved to California and says it has changed her life). It will keep the frame in place if it wasn't quite level—and every time the door closes (or there's an earthquake) the frames won't shift and get lopsided. It's especially helpful when you're doing a collage, where things just look messy if they get crooked.

A word about photo collages:

Bigger is better when it comes to collages, and pretty much wall art in general. The tinier your frames get, the more cluttered your house is going to feel. That's not to say you can't hang a small photo here or there, it's just better to do seven big frames than fifteen small frames for a collage. And you usually want uneven numbers when grouping photos together. And definitely use the painter's-tape trick to see where you want everything to go and what looks best where.

Bonus

Jasmine's art rule: Every room, even the bathroom, should have some framed personal photos on display. They don't need to be professional photos. Frame a selfie, a candid shot, or a picture of your dog with its tongue out—anything that makes you happy. The funny "Oh my god, remember what happened when we took this photo?" ones often tell more of a story than posed professional shots.

Pro tip: If you want to blow up and frame a black-and-white photo, but you don't want to pay crazy money for it, you can have it printed at an office supply store as an "architectural print" on regular paper instead of photo paper. When you put it in the frame behind glass, it looks great and it will cost you about one dollar!

PATCH A SMALL HOLE IN THE WALL

1. Get a small container of spackle, a spackling knife, and a sanding block (readily available at hardware stores).

2. Put a little spackle on your knife and work it into the hole as if you're buttering toast, filling in the nooks by spreading the spackle back and forth.

3. Make sure the hole is completely filled, and scrape any excess spackle off with the knife (held at about a 45-degree angle).

4. Let the spackle dry—this can take up to 12 hours depending on the humidity and the size of the hole. Read the instructions on the container, as each spackle compound varies.

5. Gently sand around the spackled area with a sanding block to smooth out any ridges (the wall should be smooth to the touch).

6. Wipe down the wall with a slightly damp cloth to get rid of lingering dust.

7. Repeat the steps if needed. (Run your fingers over the job and if you can feel the spackle has recessed, you'll need a little more.)

THE EXPERT:

Jasmine Roth is the host of HGTV's *Hidden Potential* and the winner of HGTV's *Rock the Block*. On *Hidden Potential*, she transforms builder-basic houses into custom dream homes. She also founded and runs Built Custom Homes, which manages the design of ground-up residential new-construction projects in Huntington Beach, California.

THE EXPLANATION:

Patching a little nail or screw hole in drywall makes the idea of hanging a photo much more manageable—it's suddenly OK if you mess up! Larger holes—like the one my brother-in-law's butt put in my basement wall when he went diving for a Ping-Pong ball over Thanksgiving—may require patches and are better handled by pros (in my case, my dad). Painters can fix holes in the wall, so there's no need to hire a separate handyman. For a small hole, from a nail or a screw, you can easily DIY. Don't use too much spackle (you want it in the hole, not all over the wall) and be sure to wipe off any dust before painting over it. When done properly, the hole and your handiwork should disappear.

Pro tip: If you don't have spackle and you're really in a pinch, the trade secret is to use some white toothpaste. Just take a bit on your fingertip and push it into the hole. Smooth it out and let it dry. If your wall isn't white, take a little bit of the wall paint on your finger and tap it on the wall to cover the dry toothpaste, almost like you're applying concealer.

BUY A HOUSEPLANT (AND KEEP IT ALIVE)

"People aren't born with black thumbs or green thumbs; the difference is the person who says they have a green thumb is someone who has decided to put in the work. Everyone can have a green thumb."

—Hilton Carter

1. Pay attention to what type of light you have in your space— where does it come from, what rooms have the most, how big are your windows. You will also want to know which direction your windows face (no judgment if you have to use your compass app for this step).
2. Think about the type of person you are. Do you have the time and level of commitment/interest to dig in and fully understand what it takes to care for a particular plant? Be honest here.
3. Jot down a few notes about your home—"I live in a NYC apartment with windows that face west but my windows face another building." Or, "My house has big south-facing windows, but outside of those windows are big trees."

4. Go to the nursery with your notes and ask them what type of plant will do best given all the information you presented them with. Also note if you have pets—some plants are toxic to our fur friends.

5. Before you leave, ask them how best to care for the plant (e.g., how often and how much to water it, how much light it needs) and *actually listen*. Better yet, write it down.

6. When you get home, don't immediately repot the plant. Put it in the place where it will live in your home and let it acclimate. You may see a bit of leaf loss—some of the more mature leaves from the base will turn yellow or brown and fall off—but that's normal, so don't panic. Don't repot it until you see the roots coming out of the drainage holes.

7. Check to see if the plant needs water. Most only want to be watered when the top two inches are dry, so do a finger test—stick your index finger two inches into the dirt; if it's dry, give it water.

8. When watering, take it slow and be deliberate (don't just dump your half-drunk water glass in as you pass by—whoops!). Use lukewarm water (cold water shocks the roots) and pour carefully, allowing the water to seep in until it comes trickling out of the drainage holes.

9. Let the water collect in the base tray for 15–20 minutes and then drain it. If it's a big plant that you can't move easily, blot the water out of the tray with a towel or use a turkey baster. Just be sure you don't leave the water sitting there (it'll cause root rot, and that's no good).

10. Wipe down the leaves every three weeks with a damp cloth (keeping the surface clean of dust and pests allows the plant tissue to better connect with the sun).

THE EXPERT:

Hilton Carter is Apartment Therapy's "The Plant Doctor" and author of *Wild at Home: How to Style and Care for Beautiful Plants* and

Wild Interiors: Beautiful Plants in Beautiful Spaces. He has more than two hundred plants in his Baltimore apartment.

THE EXPLANATION:

You can't just say, "I have an empty corner that needs something green," or pick up a plant because you saw it all over Instagram—I'm looking at you, fiddle leaf fig! You've got to have some self and space awareness. Some plants need filtered light only, while some need direct sun. You don't want to mix this up. The acclimating step is important as the plant adapts to its new life with less light, less care, and less love than it was getting from the professionals at the nursery (no offense). And be super thoughtful about your watering. One of the biggest causes of plant death is helicopter parenting through overwatering. In general, yellow leaves are from overwatering; brown tips are from underwatering. When it gets colder out, be mindful of any drafts near your windows and pull the plants back if it feels too cold.

Bonus

Give the plant a name. Silly? Maybe. But it's a great way to get yourself onboard for the level of care it requires to be a plant owner. Throwing out a red mum that was neglected may seem OK, but throwing out Bob?! You monster! Talk to your plants ("What's up, Bob, are you thirsty today?") and spend time with them. When you're having a baby, or getting a pet, you buy the parenting books, you take the classes, you do your research and prep work so these things can live the best life possible. It's the same with plants—they're living things not just decorations.

A word about orchids:

People think they've killed an orchid when the flower dies. That's not the plant, that's just the flower! Don't toss the orchid—you can get it to flower again with a little TLC.

Bonus
......

Ready to Repot? Here Are Hilton's Tips:

1. Find a pot that's two inches in diameter *larger* than the plant's current home.
2. Fill the new pot ⅓ of the way with fresh potting mix.
3. Hold the old pot over the new pot and gently remove the plant from the old container, letting any dirt fall into the new pot. (If your plant is still in one of the flimsy plastic nursery pots, give it a little squeeze first to loosen up the soil.)
4. Gently break up the roots and soil of the plant with your hands and place it into the new pot.
5. Add some fresh soil on top and pat it down a bit, leaving about a one-inch lip on the top so it doesn't overflow when you water. (Make sure you get the right potting mix for your specific plant; succulents in particular have a special soil you can buy.) Then only water the plant if it needs it!

MAINTAIN YOUR LAWN

"Your lawn is the only living part of your asset, so you have to treat it differently, not like any other household chore."

—Allyn Hane

1. Mow frequently—at least once a week but up to 2 times in the rainy season. You never want to remove more than ⅓ of the grass blade's length in a single mowing.
2. Make sure your mower blade is sharp so you get a clean cut. (If grass tips are being shredded, it allows disease to enter the plant—like an open wound with a human.)

3. Leave the clippings on the lawn. If you have a quality mower and you're mowing often—and the clippings aren't clumping—return them to the lawn. They contain nutrients, so it's very ecofriendly.

4. Rake up leaves. If there are too many lying on the grass, they block sunlight and compete with the lawn. If there's only a smattering, it's OK for them to be mowed and mulched with the grass.

5. Water (in the morning). A general rule: Lawns need about 1 inch per week, though this will vary depending on your type of grass.

6. Fertilize every 4–6 weeks. Hardware and big box stores carry organic options, and your local garden center may be even better equipped with natural products targeted for your particular soil type.

7. Put down preemergent weed control in the early spring to prevent crabgrass.

8. Treat weeds postemergence, as needed. (There isn't a preventative herbicide for every type of weed—like dandelions, for example—so you have to deal with those as they come up, whack-a-mole style.)

THE EXPERT:

Allyn Hane is a lawn-care expert and "the Lawn Care Nut" on YouTube. His weekly show teaches DIYers how to dominate their street with the greenest, thickest, most beautiful lawn on the block. For fifteen years, he worked for TruGreen, the world's largest lawn service.

THE EXPLANATION:

The most important thing you can do for your lawn is to mow it correctly. If you don't get that right, your lawn will always be a struggle. Think of grass blades like satellite dishes soaking up signals from the sun. You want to keep them under control (not too tall) but don't cut them completely off—hence the ⅓ rule, which still leaves plenty of green for photosynthesis. The thinking on fertilizer used to be blast it once in the spring and once in the fall with massive amounts of synthetic fertilizer. Turns out it's better to "spoon-feed" small amounts of organic fertilizer more often. (There will be times when the lawn is thin or unhealthy and needs extra help, and it's OK to go on a bulking cycle then.) There are two ways to attack weeds: (1) Prevent them from ever appearing; crabgrass starts coming up when spring soil temperatures reach fifty-five degrees, so get it on your lawn before then to create a barrier in the soil. (2) Buy premixed weed control and spot spray dandelions or clover, or whatever pops up as the weather gets warmer.

A word about watering:

When you water in the morning, the sun comes up and dries it off. If you water at night, especially during humid times of year, the water will sit on the lawn all night, which can cause disease. (That said, it's better to water in the evening than not at all.) To figure out how much an inch is, take the tuna can challenge: Put an empty tuna can or two out in your yard, turn on the sprinklers, and set your timer. When the can is full, look at your timer—*that's* how long you need to run the sprinkler each week. Break that time into two days of waterings of a half inch each, say Wednesday and Sunday. If you water every single day, the roots will stay close to the surface and you'll have a shallow-rooted lawn. You want the roots to go down deep in that soil where it's cooler, to keep the plant regulated. The one exception: When you're trying to get new grass seed to grow you want to keep it constantly wet every day, for about twenty days.

WATER YOUR GARDEN

1. Check the weather to make sure no rain is predicted for the next 12 to 24 hours.
2. If no rain is coming, get outside by 7:30 or 8:00 a.m.
3. Turn on the hose and drag it to the area you want to water (trying not to crush any plants in the process).
4. Put the nozzle on the "shower" setting then turn on the hose and give each plant a good soaking, mimicking a 1- to 2-inch rainfall.
5. Spend extra time on anything newly planted. (The new stuff should be watered 5 times a week, whereas perennial shrubs and trees only need about 2–3 times, depending on the climate.)
6. Aim the hose from the base of the plant all the way out to the "drip line" (that's the umbrella of where the branches reach out to—i.e., the point on the ground where water will drip down from the widest-reaching branch of the plant).

THE EXPERT:

Chris Lambton is the host of DIY Network's *Lawn and Order* and *Yard Crashers*, and a regular on HGTV's *Going Yard*. He's based in Cape Cod, where he runs the family's landscape business, E. Lambton Landscaping. He lives there with his wife, Peyton, and two children, Lyla and Hayes.

THE EXPLANATION:

One good day of natural rain is worth three or four waterings (by you or your irrigation system), so if weather is coming skip the hose—and pull any potted plants out from under the eaves of your house. And depending on the plants, if you get a good rain that means you have the next couple of days off from watering. When you do water, do it before the ground and plants are hot from the sun. If you wait until, say, 2:00 p.m., the water will hit the plants and evaporate before it hydrates—and when it evaporates, it will burn the flower. If you water at night your garden will stay wet, which can lead to root rot. (The optimal time to set your irrigation system to go off is 5:30 a.m.) And don't obsess about watering right at the base—a plant's roots go out as far as the plant does, so you can water all the way to the drip line.

Pro tip: If you're not a huge fan of watering (or don't trust yourself with living things), stick to native flowers and plants. They don't require as much watering because they're used to the temperature and soil type and rate of rain in your area.(Google "native plant databases" for your region).

Bonus

If you're going away and worried about potted plants (they dry out faster), try this fun hack: Fill an empty wine bottle with water and put it upside down in the pot. The water will slowly seep out into the soil over time. You can also poke holes in a soda bottle or small water bottle (depending on the size of your pot), bury it so the top is sticking out a bit, and then fill the bottle with water. Of course it depends on the size of your plant, but the wine bottle will give you a couple weeks, as will the plastic water bottle.

PREVENT (AND DEAL WITH) WEEDS IN YOUR FLOWER BEDS

1. Put down 4–6 inches of mulch right after you've planted your shrubs and flowers. It's also fine to mulch over bulbs, as it provides a nice blanket for them in the winter, and when it breaks down it will help fertilize them, too.
2. When weeds inevitably pop up, wait for the day *after* rain to start pulling them.

3. Grab a bucket or an empty plastic pot (save a couple of the ones the plants came in for this purpose) and a small pointed shovel or hand trowel.

4. Designate a 5-foot square area (you can say "from this rose bush to that hydrangea") and focus *only* on that spot.

5. Pull up the weeds *with* the roots, using your tools if needed, and toss them in the bucket. (Take a work call or listen to a podcast while you weed.)

6. When the first area is completely weeded, step back and admire your work then move on to another 5-foot area, or call it a day and come back out tomorrow.

THE EXPERT:

Chris Lambton is the host of DIY Network's *Lawn and Order* and *Yard Crashers*, and a regular on HGTV's *Going Yard*. He's based in Cape Cod where he runs the family's landscape business, E. Lambton Landscaping. The company was named for his father, who used to pay Chris and his siblings a quarter for every dandelion they removed from their lawn (using a steak knife to ensure they got the root). He lives there with his wife, Peyton, and two children, Lyla and Hayes.

THE EXPLANATION:

The best thing you can do for your yard is mulch. (Have a landscaping company deliver a yard of it—a "yard" is a unit of measure; one yard of mulch is three cubic feet, and it's more economical than paying for individual bags.) As mulch breaks down, it turns into compost, which turns into heat that burns the weeds before they even start. You'll still get weeds from squirrels and birds dropping spores, so those are the ones you have to attack (they'll steal the water and nutrients from your flowers if you leave them). Rain softens the soil and makes it easier to get the weed from the root— which is necessary, otherwise it'll be back in a week. But don't just start mindlessly picking without a plan. Breaking the project into five-foot areas means you'll never be overwhelmed with the job—and you'll get immediate gratification when you see the difference you've made (which will inspire you to keep going). You can apply this same method to your driveway or patio.

Pro tip: If you don't want to wear gloves (Chris never does; it's easier without them), prevent dirt from getting under your fingernails by grabbing a bar of soap and scraping your nails on it. The soap gets under your nails so the soil can't!

BUILD A FIRE IN A FIREPLACE

1. Open the flue damper (the flue is the pipe that runs up the chimney—the damper is the flap at the bottom of the flue that opens and closes).
2. Clear the ashes from under the grate if there's a pileup. If the fireplace has been used recently, assume that the ashes are smoldering and dispose of them safely.
3. Crumple up pieces of newspaper or other easily combustible material and put them on the grate (paper grocery bags work well, and burning them for warmth will assuage any guilt you had about forgetting your reusable bags again).
4. Place a layer of kindling on top of the newspaper—kindling is small pieces of wood, sticks, or "leftover lumber" for those of us with leftover lumber lying around (just be sure it isn't pressure treated or coated with lead paint).
5. Lay small pieces of firewood at random angles covering the paper, but leaving spaces between the logs.
6. Stack larger logs on top of the smaller ones, again leaving space between each piece.

7. Roll up a few pieces of newspaper like a torch and light one end. Hold the paper up the chimney for about thirty seconds until you see the smoke rising from the paper.

8. Using a match (or the same paper torch if it's still burning), light the paper under the logs.

THE EXPERT:

John Zammett is my dad. He's been building roaring fires for sixty-five years—we used to split our own firewood when I was little, and he's never met a piece of scrap wood he couldn't turn into kindling. (He would be horrified to know how many Duraflame logs I go through in a winter.)

THE EXPLANATION:

Opening the flue is the most important step (mess this up once and you'll see why) so checking that off first means you'll always know it's done. It can be difficult to tell for sure with some dampers, so if you're new to making fires in a particular fireplace, don't skip step 7. And if it's very cold or windy, wait until just before step 7 to open the flue (cold air descends and it can force smoke into the house when you light the fire). You want good airflow under the grate—fire requires oxygen—which is why you clear big ash piles that may hinder that. Holding the torch up the chimney warms the inside and starts the air flowing up, drawing oxygen to the flames (it's also a good way to check if your flue is open). There are many ways to place wood for a fire, but this method allows the smaller logs to catch first and help get the bigger ones going.

Pro tip: Opening a nearby window can accelerate the fire-starting process because it allows the flames to pull more oxygen. If the fire is smoking heavily it means there's incomplete combustion—the more smoke you have, the less the material is actually burning (in other words, a smoky fire is not a successful one—it will also make your hair, clothes, and house smell like campfire for days).

DINNERTIME

STORE AND WASH PRODUCE

1. Don't wash any of your produce until you're ready to eat it or cook with it.

2. Dump berries (unwashed) into a paper-towel-lined glass container (brown paper towel is ideal here; white ones are bleached and you don't want that touching your food if you can help it), top with another paper towel, cover, and store in the refrigerator.

3. Store big bags of greens in the bottom drawers of the refrigerator where they'll stay freshest.

4. Refrigerate apples (they don't keep as long on the counter).

5. Take mushrooms out of plastic containers and store in brown paper bags in the refrigerator.

6. Store counter vegetables—onions, garlic, avocado—on flat trays instead of bowls; tiered tray stands work well and look pretty. (When you put a lot of fruits and veggies together in big bowls on the counter, things fall to the bottom and often get forgotten—oh, hello, shriveled old clementine!)

7. As soon as avocados get soft, pop them in the refrigerator (they'll keep for an extra 2–3 days).

8. When you're ready to eat or cook, wash your hands and *then* wash your produce.

9. Spray your fruit or vegetable with a veggie wash or use a mixture of vinegar and water (three parts water to one part vinegar, in a spray bottle, is a great DIY way to remove pesticides and residue); rinse completely with cool water, scrubbing any dirt off with your hands or a vegetable brush.

10. Rinse salad greens with cool water and, if you have one, use a salad spinner (if you have a salad spinner *and* kids, they generally love to use it, so put them on this task).

THE EXPERT:

Catherine McCord is a food expert and founder of the Weelicious brand, a trusted content resource (and gorgeous Instagram) focused on family and food. She's the author of *Smoothie Project*, *Weelicious*, and *Weelicious Lunches*.

THE EXPLANATION:

When you get home from the farmer's market or grocery store, take things out of any plastic or cardboard containers. You want to keep your produce dry until you're ready to use it—especially berries (and especially raspberries, which are really porous). Berries are like sponges and absorb any liquid you put on them, so they'll mold faster if they're put away wet (the paper towel helps wick away any residual moisture). Same goes for greens and all your vegetables. And always store things so you can see them—flat trays, glass containers, clear, compostable plastic bags. Then you'll be more likely to use your fruits and veggies, which is really the bottom line here!

Pro tip: When fresh fruit or vegetables are starting to spot or become overripe, don't throw them away. Cut them into chunks, place the pieces on a parchment-lined baking sheet, freeze them overnight, then place the frozen produce into freezer bags. They'll stay fresh for up to four months. (Write down what it is and the date you froze it.)

DEFROST MEAT

1. Take meat out of the freezer the day before you want to cook it and place it on a plate in the fridge.
2. Oh, wait, you forgot? Submerge the vacuum-sealed meat, still in the plastic, in a big bowl of tepid water for thirty minutes (you can change out the water if it gets too cool).
3. Do not microwave it. Not even on the defrost setting. Just don't. (Meats are stored in plastic; if you microwave it, that plastic will interact with whatever you're defrosting and you will be eating plastic with your meat.)
4. If you're making whole chicken, you can remove the packaging and run cold water through the body cavity to help it defrost faster.
5. Once it's defrosted, do a smell test to check whether the meat is good. (Chicken can sometimes have a slightly eggy or a sulfurous smell, but it should rinse off easily. If not, ditch it.)
6. Once you've thawed frozen meat, don't refreeze it unless it's cooked in a stock, soup, or sauce.

THE EXPERT:

Anya Fernald is a sustainable food expert, butcher, and the cofounder and CEO of Belcampo Meat Company, which includes a butchery, farms, and restaurants (they even host meat camps!). She has appeared as a judge on the Food Network's *Iron Chef America* and *The Next Iron Chef*, and is the author of *Home Cooked: Essential Recipes for a New Way to Cook.*

THE EXPLANATION:

OK, in an ideal world we plan our meals ahead of time and take the meat out of the freezer the day before. But how many of us remember to do that every time? In a pinch, the tepid-water trick works great (tepid means lukewarm, by the way). It's safe and it holds true for all types of meat—even bolognese sauce or chili. Just make sure your meat is in an air-/watertight package before submerging it, and definitely don't take chicken out of the package before soaking it in water because it will make the skin mushy. The freezing and thawing process doesn't hurt the nutritional profile of these foods. And if you use good-quality meat and freeze it in vacuum-sealed bags so there's no freezer burn, the taste should be the same. Anya has done side-by-side blind tastings of her meats and can't tell the difference between fresh and frozen! A general rule: The better the product is to start with, the better integrity it has through whatever type of storage you give it. If you start with crummy, corn-fed meat, it's not going to do great being frozen and thawed. The higher-quality meats have less water in them, meaning that when they freeze, the water won't form jagged ice crystals within the meat and compromise the muscle fibers, making it mushy. Some indicators of high-quality producers are "free-range" or "air chilled." Air chilled is very important with chicken; not only does it mean there isn't water in it, it also means the body temperature is left to go down to the refrigerator temperature through natural contact with air, not by dunking it in the bleach solution (yes, this is the process most chicken goes through).

Pro tip: If you're going to be freezing meat (a skill we've probably all picked up recently) it's best if it's vacuum sealed. You can have the store/butcher vacuum-seal it for you before you leave or buy already vacuum-sealed meat (just make sure there isn't a lot of water in the package). Proper packaging prevents bacteria from forming, moisture loss, and water from seeping in, which causes freezer burn. If vacuum sealing isn't an option, wrap the meat tightly in plastic (Saran wrap or a large ziplock), pressing out any bubbles. Focus on making the parts of the meat that are lean fully in contact with the plastic; for skin and fat it's not a problem if the plastic is not fully adhered—fat is less likely to get freezer burn.

Label the item (what it is and the date you're freezing it) and don't keep any meat in the freezer for longer than a year.

PREP FOR COOKING DINNER

1. Mentally run through your meal (either read the recipe all the way through, or visualize the steps if they're in your head).
2. Relax: Pour a glass of wine or a cup of tea, crank up your favorite music, or flip on a TV show in the background. If you need to preheat the oven for your recipe, do it now.
3. Position a large cutting board next to the stove. If you don't have the space, set it over the sink.
4. Place an empty bowl next to your workspace to collect discarded scraps while you work. This is your "garbage bowl" and it's game changing.
5. Find all the pots and pans and tools you'll need; put them in place.
6. Collect the ingredients and arrange them in your workspace in the order they'll be used (consult step 1, if needed).
7. Chop the vegetables that take the longest to cook first and work your way from there.
8. While things are cooking, straighten up your station and empty your garbage bowl if needed.

THE EXPERT:

Rachael Ray is a cook, author, and television personality who currently hosts the Emmy-winning syndicated daytime talk show *Rachael Ray* and Food Network's *30 Minute Meals*. She is also the founder and editorial director of *Rachael Ray In Season* magazine, and recently published her twenty-sixth cookbook, *Rachael Ray 50: Memories and Meals from a Sweet and Savory Life*, which became an instant *New York Times* bestseller.

THE EXPLANATION:

You don't want surprises while you're cooking, so walking through the meal first helps you identify which ingredients you need, any special equipment required, and what will take the longest to cook (you'll start your chopping there). It's also important to be in the proper headspace before you even turn on the stove—otherwise you won't have a successful dish and won't want to cook again anytime soon. If there are multiple dishes in your meal, collect only the ingredients for the one you're making first so you're not confusing yourself or crowding your workspace. Get everything close by, including your garbage bowl. Things will go much faster and more smoothly when you're not doubling your efforts (like going back and forth to the garbage can ten times). You really don't want to move much at all once you're cooking! The key to cooking efficiently is to have everything in its place before you start—your mise en place—so you're not having to search for the cast-iron skillet with raw chicken hands while your onions burn (been there). In order to make cleanup more efficient—and so you're not completely overwhelmed at the end—tidy up between each dish. (Rachael's husband does the dishes in their house...wouldn't you if RR was cooking for you?!)

Bonus

Before you turn on the heat under a nonstick pan, get out your oil/butter/stock and put some in the pan. If you preheat a nonstick pan without anything in it, you'll release toxins into the air and onto the pan (it's fine for cast iron or stainless steel).

MAKE A SATISFYING SALAD

1. Find a large stainless steel or other mixing bowl, one that can accommodate much more than the amount you're making.
2. Select at least two greens for the base—typically 1 leafy green (like arugula) and 1 textured, fibrous green (like kale). Make sure they're washed and completely dry and place them in the bowl.

3. Prep your vegetables in a variety of ways—shredded, chopped, diced, sliced. Place them in the bowl.

4. If you're using grains (quinoa and farro are great options) make sure they've cooled down so they're not hot, then add to the bowl.

5. Add protein (if you're making this a meal): shredded rotisserie chicken, beans, falafel, that leftover steak.

6. Stick with shaved or crumbled cheeses—parmesan, blue cheese, goat cheese, or feta work well. (If you grate or shred, it will stick to the lettuce.)

7. Sprinkle on something crunchy—nuts, seeds, tortilla chips (boost the flavor by toasting or roasting nuts and seeds first), and something chewy/sweet like dried apricots, cranberries, or cherries.

8. When you're ready to eat/serve the salad, pour dressing around the *perimeter* of the bowl. Go around 1–2 times for a light-medium dressed salad; 3–4 times around for heavy dressing.

9. Toss with a pair of salad tongs by starting underneath and folding the salad over on top of itself (like folding egg whites into batter for baking). Repeat until everything is shiny and dressed and the goodies are mixed throughout, not just sitting on top.

10. Finish with fresh herbs (chives or mint), smaller seeds (sesame or hemp), and sea salt and pepper.

THE EXPERT:

Katelyn Shannon is the chief research and development chef at Sweetgreen, an organic salad and warm-bowl eatery located in cities across the country. She creates Sweetgreen's seasonal and signature menus using fresh, sustainable, and locally sourced ingredients.

THE EXPLANATION:

You always want to be sure your salad-assembling bowl is bigger than your salad—even if you transfer it into something smaller for serving, an oversize bowl is easier to work with, and you'll actually be able to get everything mixed properly (a key to a successful salad) without bits of your handiwork flying out of the bowl. The amounts of everything you throw in is really personal preference (and based on what you have on hand), but you can apply this general formula to whatever you're pulling together. If the salad *is* the meal, you should definitely include a grain and protein; if you're making a side salad with dinner, you may not need all the steps. A textured green is important, as it keeps your salad from getting weighed down by the rest of the ingredients and the dressing. A variety of textures and flavors makes the salad more interesting and enjoyable. Just don't put anything in hot, especially if you have delicate greens that can wilt easily.

Bonus

Want to make a salad ahead of time? Just keep anything crunchy on the side and leave avocado off until the last minute (crunchy things can absorb too much moisture and lose their bite, and avocado will brown). Cover with a moist paper towel, making sure it's *touching* the salad and store it in the fridge until you're ready to serve, then add the rest of the ingredients and dress.

MAKE A SIMPLE SALAD DRESSING

"Once you master this skill you will never have to (or want to) buy dressing again."

—Katelyn Shannon

1. Plan your base, which is always three parts fat to one part acid (e.g., 1½ cups olive oil to ½ cup red wine vinegar).
2. Start with an emulsifier (dijon mustard or fresh egg yolk). An emulsifier is an agent that helps combine two or more ingredients that typically don't mix together (think oil and vinegar).

3. Add a sweetener like honey or maple syrup.
4. Build flavor with minced garlic, chopped shallot, herbs, or lemon/orange zest.
5. Place all the ingredients (except oil) in a blender or food processor and pulse a couple of times.
6. With the motor running, slowly pour in the oil until the dressing is emulsified.
7. Taste for seasoning and add salt and pepper as needed.

THE EXPERT:

Katelyn Shannon is the chief research and development chef at Sweetgreen, an organic salad and warm-bowl eatery located in cities across the country. She creates Sweetgreen's seasonal and signature menus using fresh, sustainable, and locally sourced ingredients.

THE EXPLANATION:

The classic vinaigrette ratio is 3:1 (oil:vinegar or fat:acid) but you can play with the amounts based on your personal tastes. If you want a silkier dressing use the full three parts oil; if you like it more acidic, cut back on the fat. Blending all the ingredients together before adding the oil helps to distribute the emulsifier so that when you add the oil, you'll have an easier time getting it all to combine (or emulsify). You can do this without a blender by just whisking the ingredients in a bowl and then continue whisking briskly as you slowly add the oil. Fresh dressing can keep for about five days in the refrigerator. The best way to store it is in a jar or container with an airtight lid (mason jars are perfect for this).

A word about dressing a salad:

Dressing goes on right before you serve. And what you put in your salad will dictate the type of dressing you want to use. If you have grains, avoid ranch or buttermilk, because the grains will suck up all the dressing and leave the rest of the salad a bit bland. Skip the creamy dressing when you have creamy cheeses or an avocado in there because it's just going to turn into a sloppy mess. When you're using soft ingredients, dress with something lighter, like a vinaigrette.

KATELYN'S GO-TO VINAIGRETTE

2 tbsp fresh lemon juice
2 tbsp fresh lime juice
1 tsp shallot, chopped
1 tsp dijon mustard
1 tbsp honey
½ tsp fresh lemon zest
½ tsp fresh lime zest
1 tbsp fresh herbs (dill, tarragon, or basil), chopped
¾ cup neutral oil (safflower or avocado oil work well)

(Follow the instructions above for emulsifying and seasoning—if you want to keep the lemon zest in bigger pieces, or have whole slices of shallot running through your dressing, add those at the end, after the emulsion is created.)

BOIL PERFECT PASTA

1. Fill a pot with water (about 6 quarts for 1 pound of pasta), put it on the stove, and turn the burner to high.
2. When the water comes to a boil, add about two tablespoons of salt.
3. Make sure the water returns to a high boil and add the pasta.
4. Stir the pasta to make sure it doesn't clump together.
5. Cook the pasta, uncovered, at a rolling boil and stir often to keep it from sticking.

6. While the water is boiling, put a colander in the sink.

7. Before you drain the pasta into the colander, use a ladle and reserve about a cup of the cooking water in a mug.

8. If you're adding pasta to a sauce, drain your pasta 1 to 2 minutes *before* what the package suggests for al dente because it's going to continue cooking as you mix it with the sauce.

9. When the pasta is done (taste it to be sure), pour it in the colander—or you can skip the colander and use tongs to transfer pasta directly to your sauce.

THE EXPERT:

Rachael Ray is a cook, author, and television personality who currently hosts the Emmy-winning syndicated daytime talk show *Rachael Ray* and Food Network's *30 Minute Meals*. She is also the founder and editorial director of *Rachael Ray In Season* magazine, and recently published her twenty-sixth cookbook, *Rachael Ray 50: Memories and Meals from a Sweet and Savory Life*, which became an instant *New York Times* bestseller.

THE EXPLANATION:

Making sure you have enough water and a big enough pot before you turn on the stove is key—pasta needs room to move or it'll clump (six quarts is twenty-four cups). (Fun fact: Rachael invented an oval pot just for boiling spaghetti so the long strands can be dropped in and actually fit!) And that may seem like a lot of salt, but you need to season the pasta—even if you're using sauce, you want the pasta itself to have flavor. (You salt the water *after* the water is boiling so the salt doesn't scar your pots.) And you want to season the water, too—it should taste like seawater. Think of the pasta water as an ingredient in your dish. The pasta will release some of its starch as it cooks, and that salty, starchy water makes a great thickener for sauces—pour a little onto your pasta to marry the pasta to your sauce.

MAKE A PERFECT BURGER

"To me, burgers are the quintessential sandwich, so for every component—the burger, the bun, the cheese, the condiments—there has to be some thought process behind it. You want to treat each one of those things individually and then bring them together."

—Bobby Flay

1. Choose beef with an 80:20 meat-to-fat ratio (chuck is good).
2. Assemble into patties, being careful not to overwork the meat (aim for around 6 ounces and an inch to an inch-and-a-half thickness per burger).
3. Season very liberally with salt and pepper on both sides; nothing else!
4. Press your thumb into the center of each burger to create a well; this will help the burger keep its shape while cooking.
5. Heat your pan or grill to high (a pan or cast-iron skillet is ideal so the burger cooks in its own juices rather than dripping away on an open grill).
6. Put a few drizzles of oil (canola, vegetable, safflower) into the pan. When smoke billows up, it's ready.
7. Place your burgers into the pan or onto the grill and don't mess with them; allow to sear for 2 to 2½ minutes (for a medium-rare to medium burger).
8. Resist the urge to press down on the burgers with a spatula—it will squeeze out all the juices.
9. Flip your burger and cook it on the other side for about 2 to 2½ minutes. Again, leave it alone.
10. Toast your buns if you're toasting them—in a toaster, in an oven, on the grill. (You should be toasting them.)
11. If you're doing cheese, place two slices on the burger and close the grill for about thirty seconds. If you're using a pan, add

three tablespoons of water to the pan, quickly cover it, and let it steam for 15–20 seconds.

12. Place the burger on the pretoasted buns and dress to your liking.

THE EXPERT:

Bobby Flay is an award-winning chef, restauranteur, and Food Network star (*Beat Bobby Flay*, *Bobby Flay's Barbecue Addiction*, *Iron Chef Gauntlet*, etc.). In 2008, Bobby opened his first Bobby's Burger Palace (twenty minutes from where I live on Long Island—score!) and there are now 19 BBPs across the country. He has written more than a dozen cookbooks and was the first chef to receive a star on the Hollywood Walk of Fame.

THE EXPLANATION:

A good burger starts in the grocery store with quality meat. And it has to have fat; if it's too lean (90 percent lean or more), it will be dry and won't have enough flavor. (As Bobby says, "If you're going to have a burger, just have a burger.") A lot of people overcomplicate burgers. One of the biggest mistakes is adding extra ingredients and seasoning the beef like it's meatloaf. Keep it simple! Salt and pepper is all you need. People also overwork the meat; you want some space in there to create the right texture. The grill also has to be *hot*, otherwise the burger won't sear—it will just kind of heat up and you'll wind up with a gray burger. The best way to ensure a really nice crust and a juicy, flavorful bite: a cast-iron skillet. Bobby even brings his outside to use on the grill. And the reason for the thumbprint is this: When a burger cooks, it plumps up like a football, then people take the back of a spatula and press down on it, which squeezes out all the juices (no! don't do that!). Instead, "fake out the burger" by putting a little well in the middle so when it cooks, it cooks back to its original shape and you don't have to mess with it.

Bobby's thoughts on cheese:

There are clearly a lot of different choices when it comes to cheese. Many people choose cheddar as a default. Bobby hates cheddar on a burger because "it doesn't melt well, it sweats," and all the oils in the cheese come out. His go-to: Good old American. People are often sheepish about ordering it because it's so basic, but so what? Bobby's bottom line: "Whether you're a burger lover or a professional cook, American cheese is the best. It's what everybody wants, I don't care what anybody says; it has the right flavor and it reminds you of your childhood, and that's what burgers are all about."

Bobby's thoughts on burger buns:

"You can pick whatever bun you want to use as long as the texture is soft. Buying an artisanal burger bun with a firm, textured outside breaks up the burger. You want something like a potato bun or a sesame bun that's soft so when you put the burger inside, it actually becomes *part* of the burger. And I always toast it—it's that simple. You want to have that contrast in texture."

Bobby's thoughts on burger temperature:

"If you ask every professional chef how they want their burger cooked, 99 percent of them are going to say medium rare, and then a few people are going to say rare. I want my burger *medium* and I'll tell you why. It's not a steak, it's not a filet mignon; there's a difference. When a burger is at medium rare, a lot of times, the fat hasn't been given a chance to melt. You want the fat to melt a little bit, so it starts to lubricate the burger itself, on the inside. A half a step past medium rare is perfect for a burger."

PACK UP LEFTOVERS

"Don't think of leftovers as the same meal reheated, think of them as potential ingredients for entirely new dishes."
—Dan Pashman

1. Transport the leftovers to safety before stuff you wanted to save gets scraped into the garbage. (This is especially important if you're entertaining, and someone dashes into the kitchen trying to be helpful.)

2. Find the appropriate-size containers for the amount of each food you want to save and lay them on the counter (skip the plastic bags; they're bad for the environment and, well, how many people do you know who like to eat out of bags?). Also find the corresponding tops. I know, I know, easier said than done.

3. Think about what the leftover's second life will look like and do a little prep work—is the meatloaf becoming sandwiches? Slice it now while the cutting board is still out and the kitchen's already a mess. Shred the chicken tonight for tacos tomorrow.

4. If the leftover food is still hot—and it's something with a crisp you want to maintain (breaded chicken or, say, apple crisp)—let it cool completely before packing. Otherwise you don't need to wait for things to cool.

5. Combine like items to help fill containers (vegetables that may get tossed together for an omelet, beans and rice that will wind up being stirred together anyway), but keep pasta and sauce separate.

6. Are you bringing this stuff to work for lunch tomorrow? Take a minute to assemble that now.

7. Store your food in the front of the fridge where you can easily see it—there's nothing sadder than leftovers you totally would have eaten if only you hadn't forgotten they were in there.

THE EXPERT:

Dan Pashman is the creator and host of the James Beard Award–winning food podcast *The Sporkful*. (Dan says, "It's not for foodies, it's for eaters." He and his guests obsess over the details of eating to uncover truths about food and people.) He also hosts Cooking Channel's *You're Eating It Wrong* and is the author of *Eat More Better: How to Make Every Bite More Delicious*. (Full disclosure: His daughter and my daughter were in the same fourth-grade class.)

THE EXPLANATION:

The success of leftovers lies in the containers you store them in. The less air you have in there the longer the food will keep, so you want the containers to be full. A container full of food also looks more appealing than one that's 75 percent empty. Glass is best, as you can put it in the dishwasher, it's easy to clean, and it's not plastic. Go for flat containers with hard flat tops so you can stack them. If something is hot when you pack it, it's going to create steam, which will turn into condensation inside the container. Trapping that moisture inside isn't necessarily bad (unless it's a dish that needs to be crispy) and can actually help keep the dish from drying out when reheated. Bottom line: The better the food is packed away the more likely you are to use it.

Bonus

The key to *enjoying* leftovers: Pull them out of the fridge at least an hour before you plan to eat them so they can come to room temperature. They'll be more appetizing to work with when whatever fat was in there isn't congealed and then you won't have to reheat things too much and run the risk of overcooking. Take steak, for example. If you like it medium rare, bringing it to room temp means you won't turn it into a hockey puck trying to warm it up (you could even eat it room temp in a sandwich).

FIGURE OUT WHERE TO EAT

"Remember, the restaurant you pick is going to tell a little bit of a story about you, so you have to think it through."
—Chris Stang

1. Think about the overall experience you're looking for (the vibe you want on a first date will be different from a birthday celebration with old friends).
2. Consider noise—it's one of the things that can most ruin the restaurant experience, so it's really important to know what the decibel level will be regardless of who you're dining with.
3. Now think through the various food options (check out the menus online)—and, more important, will they work for everybody in your party. Asking people about dietary restrictions is pretty much a prerequisite across the board these days.
4. Read reviews, but don't just focus on the food; look for clues that check the boxes you're looking to check from steps 1 and 2.
5. When in doubt, call the restaurant and ask questions. (Do they have a kids menu? Are there gluten-free options? Will there be a guy with a guitar doing really loud Phil Collins covers?)
6. If you're planning ahead, make a couple reservations then ask the others you're going out with to help you decide, just be sure to cancel any reservations you won't be using. *Always.* (And don't wait until the day of.)
7. Know that there is nothing wrong with going back to the same restaurants again and again.

THE EXPERT:

Chris Stang is the cofounder of The Infatuation, a restaurant discovery platform (they have mobile apps, a newsletter, a text service, and a website) that covers more than three dozen global cities. They have a unique approach to creating and delivering restaurant guides (one of their lists is "where to eat with your third-tier friends"). In March 2018, The Infatuation acquired legendary restaurant review brand Zagat. Chris is also the coauthor of *How to Drink Wine*. SEE PAGE 147 FOR THOSE TIPS!

THE EXPLANATION:

It's not about going to the restaurant with the hottest chef, or the most frequently photographed food, it's about finding a great restaurant that's going to fit all your particular needs on that particular night (and yes, those needs may have changed after months and months of *not* being able to eat out). The food is obviously important, but there's always a series of parameters to consider and then you back the best restaurant into those parameters. It starts with location and what's convenient and doable for everyone in your party. (If you're driving, what's the parking situation?) And if it's an intimate date or a business dinner—or you just don't like loud restaurants—you want to be sure the noise won't be an issue. The more you know about what you're going to get when you get there (from the food to the music to the service) the better. Which is why revisiting favorites works.

Bonus

Going out in a group? If you're going out with a group of, say, five or more, find a restaurant with a round table—call ahead and ask if they have one and reserve it. Then you can at least all pretend you're having the same conversation!

Going out on a date? For a first date, pick a place you know pretty well so you can recommend things off the menu or order a bottle of wine you've had before. The more knowledgeable you seem, the better that date will go (and you won't accidentally wind up at a place with communal tables or quiet romantic vibes). Find a place with a great bar that you can sit at and then move to a dinner table if you want. But no pressure.

Going out for a business dinner? These are people who would not normally be going out together, which means your interests (culinary and otherwise) may be vastly different. Look for variety on the menu, ask ahead about any dietary restrictions, and definitely consider noise and table size if you'll be pulling out paperwork.

A word about being the one to pick the restaurant:

"The ability to choose a great restaurant, for any situation, gives you social capital. And social capital is one of the most valuable things to people—who doesn't want to be the person on a date or in a group of friends or at work who can choose the perfect place to eat or order the perfect bottle of wine?" —Chris Stang

EAT AT A RESTAURANT (WHEN YOU'VE GOT LITTLE KIDS WITH YOU)

1. Call ahead (or check their website) and see how family friendly they are. Hint: It's not a great sign if they don't have a children's menu, but it doesn't mean they won't accommodate you.
2. If you're going for dinner, go on the early side when the restaurant will be quieter, the waitstaff will be less frazzled, and you won't cut into bedtime.
3. Ask for a corner table rather than one in the middle of the room where you'll be on display. (Booths are good for little-littles so you can hug up close to keep them seated.)
4. As soon as your server shows up, set expectations and let them know your plan—that you want to order the kids' meals right away, say, while you have a drink and peruse the menu.

5. Let your kids order some special items they don't usually get at home so they understand that eating out is a treat (and they should bring their A-game behavior).

6. If kids are starving, ask for bread or chips or something quick off the menu that can keep their blood sugar (and behavior) in check while their food is being prepared.

7. When the adults order, ask the server to bring your child's dessert at the same time as your meal (dessert comes with the kids' meals at many restaurants).

8. If they get restless, take a walk to the bathroom to wash hands.

9. When the adult food is served, ask for the check. You don't have to pay it right away, but the option is there if the wheels come off and you have to eat and run.

10. Tidy major messes before you go—or just leave a bigger tip.

THE EXPERT:

Karalee Fallert is the owner of All Good Industries in Charleston, South Carolina, which includes the restaurants the Park Cafe, the Royal American, Taco Boy, and Wiki Wiki Sandbar. She also founded a Montessori Learning Center and the Green Heart Project, a community-based volunteer organization that integrates school farms as outdoor classrooms.

THE EXPLANATION:

A little bit of prep work can make this a more enjoyable experience for everyone involved. Reach out in advance and say, "Can you help me navigate your restaurant with my children?" Communicating with the staff is huge—they don't want you to be stressed any more than you want to be stressed. Staggering the meals is key to optimize your own enjoyment—when kids' food arrives first, you can cut it for them, and help them get settled without sacrificing your own dish. Then they can be occupied with ice cream while you eat your dinner. When it comes to taking little kids to restaurants, begin with the end in mind. How do you want them to ultimately behave in a restaurant? Even at a young age they're absorbing more than you think, so pay attention to table manners, noise level, and being kind to the servers (e.g., if there are french fries all over the floor, pick them up so your child understands that this is someone else's space and you need to be respectful).

SEEM LIKE YOU CAN NAVIGATE A RESTAURANT'S WINE LIST (EVEN IF YOU CAN'T)

1. If there's a wine list in your hand, it's because someone in that restaurant chose the wines that are on it. Ask them for help.
2. Start by indicating to them how much you want to spend. Be direct, even if it's $40. Good restaurants take pride in having good value on their list, and the sommelier/wine person will be glad you told them regardless of your budget. (You can point to the dollar amount you want to spend on the menu and say "something in this range" if you want to be discreet.)
3. Decide on a general category: red, white, sparkling, rosé, etc.
4. Pick a country or large wine-producing region. If you are unsure, play it safe and say France or California for the sake of simplicity and because you'll find bottles from both on almost every list. Italy is safe, too, but follow-up questions may be tough to answer because there are so many grapes and regions there.
5. Choose either a style or a grape varietal.
   Style = light, medium, full-bodied.
   Grape varietal = pinot noir, chardonnay, sauvignon blanc, etc.
6. Be confident. Even if you have no idea what you're saying.
7. Ask for input. Leaving it open-ended allows for the wine person to help guide you. It should sound something like this:

"I'm looking for something in the $70 range, red, from California. Preferably on the lighter side. Happy to hear your suggestions…"

8. Never pronounce a "t" just to be safe.

THE EXPERTS:

Chris Stang is the cofounder of The Infatuation, and Grant Reynolds is an award-winning sommelier and owner of Parcelle Wine in New York City. Their book *How To Drink Wine: The Easiest Way To Learn What You Like* covers everything from how wine is made to whether or not it really needs to "breathe" to why you should stop drinking pinot grigio (sorry, Aunt Kathie).

THE EXPLANATION:

A good sommelier will appreciate your ability to articulate the basic things you're looking for, and should be able to lead you to a bottle you'll enjoy. Even a staffer with minimal wine knowledge should be able to bring you relatively close to something you'll like. If no one is around who knows what they're talking about, it probably doesn't matter what you choose from that list. Close your eyes and point at something. Or maybe have a beer instead. Seriously, though, when you can confidently discuss a wine list and come to a decision, the person sitting across from you will be impressed with your ability to take control of the situation, even if you do end up confessing that you have no idea what exactly the two of you are currently drinking. Confidence is 90 percent of the game. In wine and in life.

Bonus

Some "always safe" bets you'll find on most any list:

Champagne
Chablis

White Burgundy
Italian white (NOT pinot grigio)
Barbera
Beaujolais
Chianti
Côtes du Rhône
Santa Barbara pinot noir

HOSTING (AND GUESTING)

PLAN A COCKTAIL PARTY

"Put the music on, fix yourself a gimlet, and enjoy the ritual of the set-up as much as you hope to enjoy the actual party. The more love and fun that goes into the planning the more love and fun your guests will feel throughout the night."

—Mary Giuliani

1. Come up with a food theme to help make the party cohesive (and the planning easier). Don't serve Mexican bean dip next to a tray of sushi. If you're going bean dip, do quesadillas or taquitos. This will also help you choose your drink (margaritas, baby!).

2. Make sure everything you're serving requires no more than one small plate, one fork, and one cocktail napkin. If it's larger than that, skip it.

3. If you have an ice maker, start bagging ice a few days before the party so you have enough. (Throw a package of pigs in a blanket in the freezer, too, just in case.)

4. Shop for your bar. You probably know what your guests like, but here are the basics: white wine, red wine, vodka, gin, tequila, scotch, sparkling water, tonic, cranberry juice (white

cranberry if you want to avoid stains), and ice. Plus lemons and limes for garnish.

5. If you're doing a signature cocktail, make a big batch of it ahead of time and serve it in a punch bowl, drink dispenser, or any vessel big enough to hold it.

6. Make a playlist (20 songs max) that serves as a blueprint for the night: start slow, build up, wind down.

7. Lay out bowls, platters, and serving pieces the day before—use Post-its to show where various things will go and put away anything you don't need. This prevents you from searching for just the right bowl as guests are arriving and eliminates any extra clutter.

8. Clean all bathrooms (even the upstairs one you don't think anyone will use). Empty wastebaskets, make sure you have toilet paper and hand towels, and place a scented candle.

9. Empty your dishwasher and trash can. (Put extra garbage bags in the bottom for easy replacement.)

10. Decide where the coats will go—a bed, a rack you put in the hallway, a cleaned-out hall closet.

11. Set up your bar area. If you'll continue to cook/prep when your guests arrive, set it in the kitchen. Cut the lemons and limes. Chill white wine one hour before your guests arrive.

12. Light the candles, take a deep breath, and do a quick walk-through of your party from start to finish from the perspective of your guests to make sure you've got everything covered. Turn on the playlist and you're ready.

THE EXPERT:

Mary Giuliani is the owner of Mary Giuliani Catering and Events (they do parties for major celebrities like, oh, Bradley Cooper). She is the author of *Tiny Hot Dogs: A Memoir in Small Bites* and *The Cocktail Party: Eat, Drink, Play, Recover.*

THE EXPLANATION:

Cocktail party entertaining means nibbles and drinks, not a formal meal, so keep it simple (if you're hosting dinner, SEE PAGE 153 FOR HOW TO SET AN IMPRESSIVE TABLE). Prepping as much as you can ahead of time means you'll be calmer come party day (and you'll sleep better the night before). Give yourself two hours before guests arrive for your preparty setup ritual. Blast some music, have some fun, make sure all the steps have been checked off. Are the bathrooms clean? Where will coats go? Where's the bar? There's nothing wrong with setting it on your kitchen island or table so if you're in there working, you won't be alone; plus it's easy access to refills! The key to making postparty cleanup go smoothly is starting with a clean house. Have to-go containers on hand and offer guests something to take home at the end of the night (the more they take, the less you have to put away). And always force yourself to clean up the night of the party—cleaning with a buzz is so much better than cleaning with a hangover.

Bonus

Here's a little cocktail party math: Doing hors d'oeuvres? Aim for four to five pieces of each item you're serving per person per hour. When buying the booze, remember this equation: Guests typically have two drinks the first hour of the party and then one drink per hour for the duration. A bottle of wine has about seven glasses per bottle; champagne has six flutes per bottle; and a bottle of liquor makes about twelve cocktails. You want two glasses per person, so if you're having ten guests, make sure you have twenty glasses on hand.

Pro tip: A cheese board can go with any themed food party, and they appeal to pretty much everyone—and it's the perfect thing to have out and ready when your guests walk in hungry—but keep it separate, not on the main food table; they work best when they stand alone. (By the bar, maybe; or on the coffee table in front of the fire.) FOR HOW TO ASSEMBLE AN INSTAGRAM-WORTHY CHEESE BOARD SEE PAGE 162.

SET A FANCY TABLE

"If the table is stunning, even if the food isn't perfect, people will
be enjoying themselves. It's not just about the food, it's about the
intimate experience of sitting down together in your home."

—Liz Curtis

1. Come up with a theme—this could be anything from an elaborate Italian feast to "blue and white."
2. Lay down your linens. A runner is all you need, unless you don't like the way your table looks, then put down a tablecloth and add a runner on top.
3. Place your napkins. Use cloth—it's a simple, inexpensive touch that won't go unnoticed—and try this technique: Fold two sides in toward each other so the napkin becomes a rectangle and lay it vertically, folds facing down, in front of each seat. The top can be touching or overlapping the runner and the bottom may be hanging off the table a little.
4. Set the plates on top of your napkin. Dinner plate, then salad plate on top (and if you're really going overboard and serving soup, the soup bowl on top of that).
5. Place the flatware—forks on the left (salad fork on the outside, dinner fork next to the plate), knife and spoon on the right (spoon on the outside of the knife, and the knife blade faces the plate). If you have a dessert spoon or fork or *both*, they lie horizontally above the plate with the handle facing the side they would go on (fork to the left; spoon to the right). Don't overcrowd your table, though—if you're not serving a course, skip the corresponding utensil.
6. Arrange glassware to the right of the dinner plate above the knife and spoon and be sure to include a water glass, which can shift to the left of the plate as you add more glasses. If you're getting really festive and you have enough for everyone,

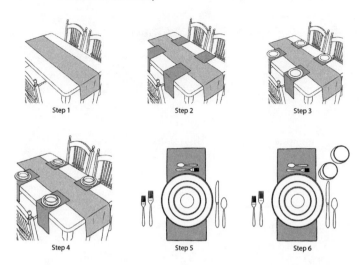

Step 1 Step 2 Step 3

Step 4 Step 5 Step 6

a champagne flute is a nice touch. If you're planning to give a toast as guests are seated, prepour a small glass of champagne. FOR HOW TO GIVE A GREAT TOAST SEE PAGE 168. Otherwise, prepouring will lead to warm, and potentially wasted, bubbly.

7. Put candlesticks with tall, tapered candles evenly spaced down the center of the table (if you're using two they should go on either side of your centerpiece) and scatter votives. Lighting the candles is the last thing you do before guests arrive so that your tapers don't melt before your meal is finished.

8. Keep flowers simple and low enough that guests can see over them. You can make your own arrangement (SEE PAGE 156) or even buy small plants to place down the middle of the table. Let guests take them home at the end of the night!

THE EXPERT:

Liz Curtis is the founder of Table + Teaspoon, a luxury table-setting rental company. (They deliver kits with everything you need to gorgeously entertain right to your front door nationwide. Once the party is over, you pack the table settings in the box they arrived in and send them away!)

THE EXPLANATION:

Linens are the foundation of the table. Runners help ground the look in a simple, sophisticated way. Cloth buffet napkins can be ordered online for about $1 apiece and come in a ton of colors. Putting them under the plates is another way to add depth and texture to the table. If you want to use napkin rings, place them on top of the plate. (Liz doesn't love putting a folded napkin to the left of the plate because it feels disjointed to have only some of the flatware on the napkin.) Someone at the table will be familiar with appropriate flatware placement, so pay attention to that step but try staggering things for a more interesting look. Forks on the left, yes, but put one an inch lower than the other and then do the same with the knife and spoon. Varying heights and shapes of glassware gives the candle light more surfaces to bounce off (and this is why you use two different heights of candles). And always fill the water glasses before guests sit down (it will encourage them to take sips of water in between sips of everything else).

Fun fact: The reason the blade of the knife faces inward: During the Anglo-Saxon period when a lot of this table etiquette stuff was being established, people would bring their own knives to dinner. Those knives were *very* sharp, so it was considered an act of aggression if you had your knife facing out toward your neighbor. (How's that for dinner party conversation?!)

A word about music:

Movie soundtracks are an excellent resource for dinner party ambient noise. *Dirty Dancing* is perfect for a playful evening, Hans Zimmer from *Pirates of the Caribbean* or *Inception* provides a more sophisticated tone, and Sofia Coppola's *Marie Antoinette* will elevate your party with a super-cool vibe.

ARRANGE FLOWERS IN A VASE

"Floral arranging uses the basic design principles of balance and alignment, which means things aren't just placed randomly; you've given thought to the order, texture, contrast, and proportion to the vase."

—Katie Hartman

1. Choose your vase. (Keep the size and shape in mind when selecting floral size and quantities.)
2. Have a general vision before you start placing the stems—will it be tight and compact? Tall and more free-flowing? Where is it going?
3. Find a clear work space with enough room to spread the flowers, clippers, and vase. Bring a garbage can over so you can brush scraps into it (or just cut stems over the can).
4. Fill the vase ¾ of the way to the top with fresh, cool water.
5. Unwrap your flowers from the packaging and toss anything dead or wilting. (You can also toss that little packet of chemicals.)
6. Clean the stems by removing any leaves with your hands or clippers (submerged leaves will breed bacteria faster and decay the flowers).
7. Hold the flower next to the vase (with the bottom of the stem on the counter) to see where you want to cut it (this will depend on the type of arrangement you're going for; the shorter you cut them, the more tightly they'll sit).
8. Cut the stems at an angle so there's more surface area for the flower to drink water (if you got them from the grocery store they probably haven't been cut in a while).
9. If using greens, place them in the vase first, crisscrossing the stems to create a grid that you'll rest your focal blooms on (if you're doing all the same flower, just start by crisscrossing a few of them).

10. Place the flowers in groups of threes—some should arch out while others get tucked in close to the vase. (If it's not a 360-degree arrangement, meaning the vase will be against a wall, put the prettiest blooms front and center.)

11. Fill in holes with any smaller accent flowers you have left.

12. Step back and determine if you need to add or reposition any blooms.

13. Change the water *daily* and give stems a fresh cut every other day to prolong the life of the arrangement.

THE EXPERT:

Katie Hartman is the founder of Floral Crush Studio, a busy event floral company in Los Angeles. Her clients include HBO, E!, Rolex, Netflix, Kate Hudson, NBC, and Facebook.

THE EXPLANATION:

Having the right vase for the job makes the process easier and more enjoyable, but it will also showcase the flowers properly—peonies, for example, look great in a wide vase so they can splay out and show off how big they get. If you have high ceilings, you want a tall vase and flowers with some height; if you want an arrangement in your bedroom, go with something small to fit your bedside table (just be sure you like the scent of the flowers). A single variety is good for a modern look and you can do pavé, which is easy and instantly gives color to a room (cut stems short so the blooms sit right at the top of the vase and pack them in tight). Or if you want more movement, cut stems different lengths and place some close to the vase and some high to draw the eye up and out. "Focal flowers" are the larger, more beautiful heads you've spent the most money on, so you really want to let them shine. You do want some white space—it makes the flowers stand out more—but eyeball it and make sure any negative space looks like it's on purpose. And never cut stems too short at first in case you need to switch things up!

Pro tip: When choosing flowers, make sure the petals are firm, not limp or soft. You can never go wrong with lilacs in the spring, peonies in early summer, dahlias in early fall, or amaryllis in the winter. Calla lilies are also good for the house, as they're elegant and last a long time, and hydrangeas are a pretty way to fill space in a big arrangement. When in doubt, monochromatic color is always chic.

BUY A GOOD BOTTLE OF WINE (FOR UNDER $20)

"The key here is knowing what you like—even just a few descriptive words about the flavors, body, or earthiness you're into will help someone guide you to a wine you'll enjoy."

—Alyssa Vitrano

1. Ask yourself what you're buying this wine for: To drink with a meal? Light appetizers? On its own?
2. Take a minute to think about what you like in a wine: Bold reds? Crisp whites with some acid?
3. If you're buying for a friend (or drinking the bottle with one), figure out what they like drinking, too.
4. Beeline to the nearest salesperson, who spends way more time tasting wines than you do and is there to help.
5. Tell them what you figured out in steps 1–3 and how much you want to spend.
6. Be open-minded. Often the lesser-known grapes and regions are less expensive but just as tasty.
7. Ask the person helping you what they're liking at the moment. It's literally their job to taste a lot of different wines, and they'll

know much more about the specific wines in their store, including the hidden gems.

8. If you need to serve a white or rosé wine right away, check out what they have available in their refrigerator.

THE EXPERT:

Alyssa Vitrano writes about wine at grapefriend.com and on her popular @grapefriend Instagram account. She has a certification in both viticulture and vinification and blind tasting from the American Sommelier Association. More importantly, she just really loves wine.

THE EXPLANATION:

Before you walk into a wine store, you should have a sense of what you like, what occasion you're buying for, and how much you want to spend. Knowing all that will make the process so much easier. Not sure what you like? Next time you're ordering a glass of wine at a bar or out at dinner, ask for a small sip of two (or even three) of the wines you're choosing between. When you're comparing wines at the same time, it's much easier to start figuring out your palette and identifying key things you like. When you get to the store, don't be shy asking for help (even at dusty wine stores, the staff tastes many or all of the wines and can guide you in the right direction); otherwise, you wander and waste time. And be wary of gravitating toward the names you know—Napa cabernets and Sonoma chardonnays often aren't the best values, since people will generally pay more for names they're familiar with and the cost of those wines are often hiked up. If you love any new wine once you try it, take a picture of the label so you remember it for next time. (Good to know: In general, American wines are named for the grape—chardonnay, sauvignon blanc, cabernet—while French and Italian wines are named by the region where the grape is grown—Chablis, Sancerre, Burgundy.)

Bonus

No one available to help? If you're looking for white, sauvignon blanc is a good grape and you can usually find one at a decent price. But instead of going French (like a Sancerre), try one from New Zealand or even South Africa—they're deliciously grapefruity and often around $15. Skip pinot grigio, which Alyssa says can often taste like wine-flavored water (can't disagree there!), and try pinot gris or pinot blanc. It's the same grape but made in different styles and has more apple notes. (Oregon pinot gris is excellent.) If you want red, go with Malbec from Argentina, an easy-drinking but bold table wine or an Oregon pinot noir. And if it's a night for bubbles, prosecco (Italian sparkling wine) is peachy and delicious. You could also go with crémant, which is made in the same method as champagne and is one of the wine world's best kept secrets.

ICE A LAYER CAKE

1. Once the cake has cooled to room temperature, chill it (still in the pans) in the refrigerator for 20 minutes.
2. Make sure your frosting is at room temperature; reserve about a cup of it in a small bowl.
3. After taking the cake out of the refrigerator, remove the layers from the pans.
4. Place cake layers on a flat surface and examine tops to see if they're too rounded to stack; if needed, make them level using a long, serrated knife.
5. Using some of the reserved frosting, put a dollop in the center of your cake plate, then stack the cake, cut sides down. Don't forget to spread frosting between layers.

6. Spread the rest of the reserved frosting all over the cake—this is your "crumb coat" and it's a game changer, folks.

7. Run a (clean, inexpensive, and used only for this purpose!) spackling knife around the cake to flatten the frosting (there will be crumbs in it and that's OK).

8. Stick the cake back in the fridge for 20 minutes.

9. Pull your cake out of the fridge and, using the remaining frosting, apply your final layer.

THE EXPERT:

Duff Goldman is a celebrity pastry chef, Food Network star (*Ace of Cakes*, *Kids' Baking Championships*), and author of *Duff Bakes* and *Super Good Baking for Kids*.

THE EXPLANATION:

Frosting a cake successfully is all about nailing the steps leading up to that final coat. When you chill a cake, the fat in it (butter, oil) solidifies, making the whole thing sturdier so clumps of cake don't peel off with the icing. And since frosting is mostly fat, if you put it on a warm cake, it'll just melt. Canned, room-temperature icing is good to go, but if you've made your own (worth it!) and it's in the fridge, warm it up while the cake chills. (Duff uses a blow torch for this step, but you can put the frosting bowl over a pot of boiling water, or just leave it on the counter for an hour or so.) Even with the cooling step, you will create some crumbs, so the essential "crumb coat" layer is just to deal with that (putting a little frosting in a separate bowl to use here means you won't crumbtaminate the main frosting bowl—if using store-bought frosting, you could just use a second can). Cooling it again firms up the crumb coat so your final layer will be easy to spread—whip out the spackle knife again if you want an extra-smooth finish.

Pro tip: Don't panic if your cake browns around the edges. People worry about overcooking, but that color gives it flavor and really good stability. The darker it is, the harder that edge will be, the easier icing will be. (And if you're using the box mix, there's a ton of, um, industrial ingredients in there to keep it from drying out.)

ARRANGE A CHEESE BOARD

1. Place the cheeses on the board—aim for a variety of milks (sheep, goat, cow), or a variety of textures (soft, hard, fresh)—then add whatever ramekins you'll be using for dips.
2. To arrange the meats, fold salami in quarters, slice hard sausages, and tear prosciutto into smaller pieces and lay in neat lines near the cheeses.
3. Add produce (carrots, cucumber, berries, dried fruits, even those cute pickles called cornichons) by placing them in "produce ponds" or piles in various areas of the board. Use a ramekin for anything in a brine or liquid.
4. Place the crunch—crackers, toasts, nuts, chips, pretzels. Fill in the gaps where the cheese and meat aren't touching with piles of nuts or fanned-out crackers. (Always do a backup plate of crackers on the side.)
5. Fill the empty ramekins with whatever dips you have planned—fig jam, honey, compote, hummus.
6. Finish with a garnish—sprigs of fresh thyme, rosemary, lavender, even edible flowers.

THE EXPERT:

Marissa Mullen is a cheese board influencer (yup, that's a thing!) and creator of the @thatcheeseplate and the @cheesebynumbers method. She's the author of *That Cheese Plate Will Change Your Life.* (Spoiler alert: It will!)

THE EXPLANATION:

Marissa's "cheese by numbers" method means you can take any ingredients you have on hand and make them look beautiful by following six basic steps: cheese, meat, produce, crunch, dips, garnish. Cheese is first and then you build around your biggest items. Precut your harder cheeses to make grazing and grabbing easier (no one wants to fumble with one of those tiny cheese knives). You want everything accessible, which is the same reason you fold the meats. The produce step is where you fill in the color, so go for a variety of fruits and vegetables—the garnish adds a final pop of color and makes the whole thing feel more artistic than a basic appetizer (make no mistake, a good cheese board IS art). You can make a cheese plate ahead of time; just cover it in plastic wrap and store in the fridge (remove crunchy items so they don't get soggy). Bring the board out an hour before serving so the cheeses can come to room temperature, where their flavors are fullest.

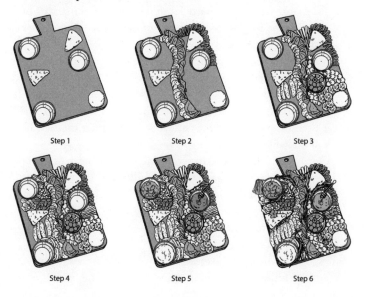

Step 1   Step 2   Step 3

Step 4   Step 5   Step 6

Bonus

Add a salami river. Marissa coined the term "salami river" to describe her style of winding stacks of folded meat around the cheese to add texture and movement. Using presliced, prepacked salami, fold each slice in quarters—stack the folded sections in your hand as you go and add a little bit of pressure. Once you have about five or six pieces, stand them up on the board and then continue to add to it, creating a line across the plate. Create the flow shape by pushing the line into a curve or two (the more you do it the easier it is, and you can do it with any type of meat).

UNCORK A BOTTLE OF WINE LIKE A PRO

1. Take your wine from the cellar or fridge and familiarize your-self with the ledge around the top of the bottle (that foil sleeve that covers the neck is called the capsule).

2. If the bottle is sparkling or white, wipe down any condensation so it isn't slippery when you're handling it.

3. Put the wine on a table or counter and grab your corkscrew. (If you don't already have one, get a "waiter's friend corkscrew"—it's the simple one with two levers and a knife; they're cheap and available everywhere.)

4. Open the knife of the corkscrew. Holding the neck of the bottle sturdy with the other hand, carefully guide the blade around the *bottom lip* of that ledge in the front, and then again around the back, scoring the foil completely around.

5. Peel off the top of the capsule, then slide it in your pocket or toss it in the trash.

6. Find the worm—the screw part of the corkscrew—put your pointer finger against the tip, and place it in the center of the

cork. Angle it down so that it will be forced to screw straight into the middle of the cork.

7. With your other hand still stabilizing the bottle, screw the cork in with your dominant hand until there is only one rung (or "staircase") of the screw left visible.

8. Make sure the top lever is squared up facing straight at the top lip of the bottle—if it's sideways you may have screwed too far or not enough, so adjust accordingly.

9. Place the top lever on the lip of the bottle, move your stabilizing hand to close around the corkscrew and the neck of the bottle, and pull up gently with your dominant hand until the lower lever is able to reach the lip.

10. Lock the second/lower lever in on the lip of the bottle and pull the corkscrew up, gently rocking from side to side if needed, until the cork slides out.

11. Take a paper towel or napkin and wipe the inside of the neck of the bottle (sometimes there's fine sediment or tartrates stuck there that you don't want in your wine).

12. In a restaurant they'd hand the cork to the guest to authenticate the bottle, but you can skip that step and just drink.

THE EXPERT:

Laura Maniec Fiorvanti is a master sommelier and the cofounder of Corkbuzz Wine Studio in New York City and Charlotte.

THE EXPLANATION:

This is not a complicated process, but it's important to take your time with each of the steps—otherwise the whole thing will be awkward and much harder to pull off. The most common mistakes people make when using a standard corkscrew are: (1) not putting the corkscrew in straight so it shreds the sides of the cork, which can break, get stuck, or get bits of cork in your wine; (2) not squaring up the lever so it slips off the bottle when you're tugging, causing

Step 1   Step 2   Step 3

Step 4   Step 5   Step 6

you to hit yourself in the face—d'oh!; and (3) pulling up too soon and too aggressively on the second lever so the cork breaks—and that piece can be more difficult to extract. But, Laura says, at the end of the day, remember: Whatever happens, if you're able to pour yourself a glass of wine, it's a success.

TASTE WINE

1. See.
2. Swirl.
3. Smell.
4. Sip.
5. Swish.

THE EXPERT:

Leslie Sbrocco is a James Beard– and Emmy Award–winning wine expert, frequent guest on the *Today* show, and author of *The Simple and Savvy Wine Guide.* She regularly samples fifty to one hundred wines a week (yes, she spits). Her show *100 Days, Drinks, Dishes and Destinations* now airs on more than two hundred PBS stations nationwide.

THE EXPLANATION:

You can't help but see the wine first so that's when you look for the color and clarity—hold the glass over a piece of white paper or tablecloth for contrast. Swirl it by putting the glass on the table and making small circles with the base of the glass flat on the table. This opens up the wine's aromas and flavors, enabling you to smell it better (it's been trapped inside the bottle for a long time and needs to breathe). If it really sticks to the sides of the glass (and has "legs" slowly trickling down) that's an indicator that it could be a sweet wine or one with high alcohol. You always smell before you taste because your nose is a much more powerful tool in identifying all the flavors. Finally, you taste different things on different places of your tongue, so moving the wine around in your mouth allows it to completely coat your palate so you can appreciate the multiple components. But you're not gargling mouthwash here; just hold the sip in your mouth, then open your mouth slightly and breathe in so the air just lightly swishes the liquid in your mouth.

Pro tip: In the United States we tend to drink our white wines too cold and our red wines too warm. When whites are overly chilled the flavors are suppressed. If you pour wine into a glass and it instantly frosts the sides of a glass the way a beer would, you know it's too cold; cup your hands around the glass to warm it quickly before tasting. Meanwhile, you want reds at cellar temperature, fifty-five to fifty-nine degrees, which softens robust or higher-alcohol wines and makes them more refreshing. Pop a room-temp bottle in the fridge an hour before serving.

GIVE A GREAT TOAST

"FDR said—be sincere, be brief, be seated—and those three Bs of toasting still hold true."

—Margaret Page

1. Set up the audience. Ask them to fill their glasses, rise, and join you in a toast. (If you're out to dinner with a few friends, there's no need to make everyone stand, but do signal that you're about to give a toast so people can fill up.)
2. Think ABC—audience before content. Is it at a work function? Will there be kids there? Should you lose the salty language?
3. Identify the purpose. Are you welcoming everyone? Are you toasting to an occasion? Are you thanking your host? Make sure what you say ties back to your purpose.
4. Keep it short (a toast should be under two minutes).
5. Give some background—introduce yourself if people don't know you, set up your relationship to the person or thing you're toasting, and establish/remind people why you're all there.
6. Don't try to be funny unless you are.
7. Avoid inside stories that the audience won't get; you want to make them feel included (ABC, baby!).
8. Whatever you're toasting (a birthday, landing a new client, a great cheese plate), include a wish for the future of it (to many healthy years ahead, to world domination, to adding a salami river next time).
9. Practice your toast. Memorize it if you can. (If you wrote it out, it's OK to bring your notes with you, but try not to read.)
10. Make eye contact with the audience. During delivery find someone whose eyes are on you and look at them, then find another pair.

THE EXPERT:

Margaret Page is the vice president of Toastmasters International, a nonprofit educational organization that teaches public speaking and leadership skills through a worldwide network of clubs. She is also an etiquette expert and the founder of Etiquette Page Enterprises and Beyond the Page Coaching and Training.

THE EXPLANATION:

A good speaker knows that it's about the audience, not themselves. That's why background can be important. You're setting the stage— "I first met Leah when we were both interns," or "This organization came into existence in 1924." (In the background you might talk about what something was in the past and then at the end of the toast you'd say your wish for what you want in the future.) A lot of advice about public speaking in general will recommend that you start with a joke. That works well for people who are funny, but not everyone is (you know who you are). Be authentic; it will be more sincere and make people more receptive to what you have to say. Always prepare for the toast and work on it—it's very difficult to raise the energy level of a room if you're reading. And toasting is all about pulling the energy of the group together, which is why standing is so powerful.

Bonus

Toast hack: Don't know what to say? Search and memorize inspirational quotes (or Irish blessings) so you're not always saying, "Here's to good health!"

Three bits of toasting etiquette:

- If you're the person being toasted, you do *not* toast to yourself. You simply look graciously at those around you and nod your head as they take a drink.

- Water is totally acceptable to toast with—poured into the wineglass or even in your water glass. It used to be considered a faux pas but it is certainly no longer. Toasting is not about consuming alcohol; it's about celebrating a person, an idea, a concept.
- Don't put your hands in your pockets—it's a sign you're hiding something (some body language experts say it's a sign you have money problems—yipes!).

A word on eye contact:

"If you're looking up that's the Ozone, if you're looking down that's the No Zone, and if you're looking straight ahead that's the Go Zone." That's a Toastmasters ditty for remembering to make eye contact. Look at someone on one side of the audience and then someone on the other side, making a connection with one person at a time. It's the natural way we speak to people, and those around them will feel it.

MAKE INTRODUCTIONS

1. Introduce people according to rank, not gender or age. So the most important person's name is said first. "Beyoncé, I'd like you to meet Erica Smith." In business, the client, guest, or visitor outranks the boss or coworker and should be introduced first.
2. Look at each person you're introducing as you say their name and say it clearly and confidently.
3. Try to provide a bit of information about each person along with their names (this can be a conversation starter: "Beyoncé just won her 400th Grammy; Erica is a middle school chorus teacher.").

4. If introducing people of equal rank, start with the older person.
5. When introducing someone to a family member, you should typically say the other person's name first: "Beyoncé, this is my dad, John Zammett."

THE EXPERT:

Patricia Rossi is an etiquette coach, international keynote speaker and NBC Daytime's national manners correspondent. Her nationally syndicated *Manners Minute* airs weekly on a number of NBC, CBS, Fox, and ABC television stations. She's Twitter's number one etiquette professional and the author of *Everyday Etiquette: How to Navigate 101 Common and Uncommon Social Situations.*

THE EXPLANATION:

Properly introducing people demonstrates professionalism and credibility. And being someone who can make introductions with ease enhances your business sense and can boost your self-confidence. It also demonstrates your insight and respect for others. That's why you can't go wrong if you lead with the most important person—it's the natural order of things and it shows honor and respect. And eye contact is always key. Everyone is so tired of staring at the tops of people's heads from them looking down at their phones. Give the introduction the respect it deserves by being fully present.

Bonus

When you're introducing *yourself*, stand up with your shoulders facing the other person, make eye contact, and say only your first name, then immediately follow it with your first and last. "Hello, I'm Erin. Erin Ruddy." This lets people hear your name twice.

GREET (OR INTRODUCE) SOMEONE WHEN YOU DON'T REMEMBER THEIR NAME

1. Come clean right away. "Oh my gosh, I'm going blank, please remind me of your name."
2. Quickly add a detail about where you've met them before (if you remember that): "I know we met at X."
3. When they say their name, you say, "Of course, _____!" and *repeat* their name.
4. Say your full name back to them.

THE EXPERT:

Diane Gottsman is a national etiquette expert and the author of *Modern Etiquette for a Better Life*. She's the founder of the Protocol School of Texas, a company specializing in executive leadership and business etiquette training.

THE EXPLANATION:

You may think you should try to preempt any awkwardness by saying your name first in the hopes that it would prompt the other person to say theirs back, but that often backfires. What if they say, "Um, yeah I know who you are we've met a million times, *hi, Erin*"? Then you're in it deep. The better approach is to be genuine and own it. Giving them details about where you've seen each other before shows that you remember *them* just not their name. Repeating their name shows respect (and will help you remember it for next time—SEE PAGE 219 FOR HOW BEST TO REMEMBER NAMES).

Bonus
. . . .

OK, but what if it's your cousin's boyfriend whom you've met a bunch of times (sorry Jason . . . or is it Josh?!) or a client you really should remember? If you have enough of a heads-up before they approach you, beeline for someone in the vicinity and, without moving your lips, ask for a lifeline (à la Meryl Streep and Anne Hathaway in *The Devil Wears Prada*). Otherwise just quickly steer the conversation past the hellos and talk about something else— "Isn't it a glorious day? Anyone else thirsty?" But don't guess, don't ask, and don't lie. And as soon as you're away from that person, go find someone to tell you their name!

PICK OUT A HOST/HOSTESS GIFT

1. Ask yourself: "Does this person entertain a lot? Do they really enjoy it?"
2. If they don't, what does this person love to do *outside* of entertaining? (Not every host/hostess needs a typical host/hostess gift.)
3. Think about how much you want to spend (similar to how you decide how much to spend on a birthday gift; it's proportionate to how well you know the person).
4. Consider the event: Are you going over for a casual Saturday night in April or for New Year's Eve featuring lobster and Veuve? Gift accordingly. That said, there's no need to go overboard; even a $10 or $15 gift is great and always appreciated!
5. If it's a bigger party, avoid bringing flowers. Sometimes bringing flowers adds one more thing for the hostess to have to do (find a vase with water while trying to answer the door and entertain guests!). You can send them the day *after* the party, though; this works especially well if you forgot to bring a hostess gift. Or bring flowers in a container/vase/vessel already filled and ready to place in the perfect spot.
6. If you're defaulting to a bottle of wine make sure your host/hostess *drinks* wine, and do a little recon to find out their favorite varietal. FOR HOW TO BUY WINE, SEE PAGE 158.

7. Think of something unexpected and fun—a bag of freshly baked cookies, coffee and pastries for the morning, a fresh loaf of bread with some great cheese. (Just make it clear that this is a gift, not something you expect them to serve right away.)

8. Wrap the gift in a way that the packaging can be used again (a cloth napkin to wrap a loaf of bread—finish it with twine—or a small succulent plant in a mug). FOR HOW TO WRAP A GIFT SEE PAGE 175.

9. Pick up extra gifts and keep them on hand for last-minute invites: beautiful candles, cheeky cocktail napkins, fun coasters.

THE EXPERT:

Joy Cho is the founder and creative director of Oh Joy! a lifestyle brand and design studio. They have a wide range of licensed products including home décor, kids, pet, and furniture collections with brands like Target, Band-Aid, and Petco. For two years in a row, Joy was named one of *Time*'s 30 Most Influential People on the internet and has the most followed account on Pinterest with almost 13 million followers.

THE EXPLANATION:

A hostess gift by definition is something a host or hostess would use in the course of entertaining. But some people love hosting, while others are just doing their best to get friends together without becoming completely unraveled in the process. Asking yourself some questions about the person you're buying for is key. If it's a friend who isn't much on entertaining but worked really hard, a pedicure gift certificate might go a long way; if it's a family party, a board game could be a perfect fit for the mood. And you don't have to go overboard. It's truly the gesture (and the thought you put into steps 1 and 2) that counts. When you bring wine as the gift, pop it in a gift bag and make sure the host knows it's for them to enjoy later, not something you are expecting them to serve (same for edible gifts—you don't want to mess with any preplanned menus).

Bonus

When should you give a hostess/host gift? When you're invited to someone's house for the first time (they just moved in or you've just become friends) or when the hostess/host is celebrating a special occasion (new job, birthday, engagement, etc.). Or if you're just really grateful that we're allowed to gather in people's homes again and you want to show that gratitude. But if you're going to someone's house for a casual hang and you've been there multiple times, you don't have to feel the pressure of bringing a gift (though in those cases Joy will often swing by the grocery store and bring a pint of great ice cream—it's never not appreciated!).

WRAP A GIFT

"Wrapping gifts doesn't have to be too stressful. If you have a handful to wrap, I might suggest pouring a glass of wine and putting on some music."

—Anna Bond

1. Gather your materials: paper, ribbon, tape, scissors, and any fun tags or decorations you have.
2. Make sure you have plenty of hard, flat space to work—dining room table, kitchen counter, floor.
3. Roll out your paper to the amount you think you'll need, then place the widest side of your gift at the cut edge. Flip the gift over toward the roll so that each side of the gift hits the paper once.

4. Give yourself 1–2 extra inches past where the box is and cut your paper from the roll there.

5. Place the gift facedown in the middle of the sheet and wrap the paper around the gift, creasing the edges along the box as you go. Use one piece of tape to secure it in the center (tape paper to paper, not paper to box).

6. Trim the paper at the two open ends of the box, leaving just enough to fold about halfway down the box ends (too much paper here makes it harder to get crisp corners).

7. Fold the top of the paper down and crease at the sides on a diagonal. Fold in the flaps like an envelope, and fold the bottom corner up (if it doesn't come to a nice point, fold the edge over for a clean crease). Secure both ends with one piece of tape. Repeat on the other side.

8. Add ribbon; wrap it around the box while it's still on the roll so you don't accidentally cut it too short. Keep bows simple (i.e., easy to untie) and cut the ends of the ribbon on a diagonal.

THE EXPERT:

Anna Bond is the cofounder and chief creative officer of Rifle Paper Co., an international stationery and lifestyle brand based in Winter Park, Florida. Rifle Paper Co.'s signature aesthetic is shaped by Anna's hand-painted illustrations.

THE EXPLANATION:

You always want to measure a sheet that's just big enough to cover the gift you're trying to wrap—too much paper makes the gift look bulky. The extra inch or two can be used to fold over the cut edges of the paper before securing them together (Anna loves this little trick to make the package look neater). Don't use too much tape and don't tape the paper to the gift, as it risks damaging the present (and makes it harder for the recipient to unwrap). Creasing the paper along the edges of the box will give you a nice clean finish.

Anna's favorite ribbons are velvet or cotton—try to have colors on hand that will match any wrapping paper design. And she always wraps the ribbon around both sides of the package.

Pro tip: If something is oddly shaped, Anna suggests trying to wrap with lightweight paper—and have fun with it. Wrap the paper around a stuffed animal and gather it all at the top, then secure it with a giant bow. Of course gift bags are always nice to have on hand for those difficult-to-wrap gifts and make things much easier. Just make sure there is enough tissue to cover the gift so it's not visible from the top. Then add a few fluffed-up sheets so the bag looks full.

A word about wrapping paper storage:

It should be practical and doesn't have to take up too much space (you don't need a dedicated wrapping room). The key is keeping all your supplies together and easy to access. Anna suggests storing wrapping rolls in one tall basket in a closet with a box of ribbons, tape, and scissors next to it (keep these scissors and tape separate from your everyday ones so you don't have to search for them every time you want to wrap). Keep greeting cards and tags in a separate box.

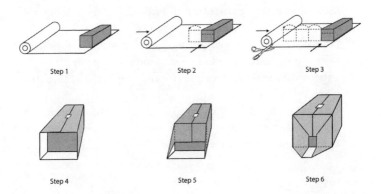

Step 1

Step 2

Step 3

Step 4

Step 5

Step 6

... 11 ...

SELF-CARE

MEDITATE

*"If you want to make your body stronger you have to move it,
but if you want to strengthen your brain you have to keep it still."*

—Suze Yalof Schwartz

1. Close your eyes.
2. Quiet the mental to-do list by being aware of your breath entering and leaving your body (putting a hand on your chest to feel it rise and fall can help).
3. Now stop thinking about your breath and just be in the moment: breathing, listening to birds chirping, hearing kids play...Whatever the moment is, tune into it.
4. Notice that you're now figuring out what to make for dinner or obsessing about that text your friend just sent, right?
5. Label what's making your mind wander—stressing, thinking, planning your piccata.
6. Bring your mind back to your breathing again, focusing on that and starting over at step 2 as needed until you can stay in that mindful moment for longer and longer stretches.

THE EXPERT:

Suze Yalof Schwartz is the founder and CEO of Unplug Meditation and author of *Unplug: A Simple Guide to Meditation for Busy Skeptics and Modern Soul Seekers* (she also developed the Unplug Meditation App, which features guided meditations and how-tos from Unplug's world-class teachers).

THE EXPLANATION:

When your mind wanders, and it will, don't push the thoughts away—they'll only come back stronger. Instead, "name it to tame it" by labeling—out loud if you have to—what's distracting you ("Sorry, chicken piccata, not now"). Then you'll be clear to get your mind and body back to the same zip code by simply noticing your breathing again. People make meditation harder than it needs to be because we think we have to turn off our brains and we can't—you actually *want* to notice how your mind wanders and what thoughts come up in your head. It's a dance between noticing how your mind works and simply placing the awareness on your breath instead of your thoughts. If you're able to consciously bring yourself back from mind wandering to mindfulness for even a minute, congratulations, you're meditating!

Bonus
....

So why is meditation such a struggle for so many people? Because we're used to having our brains distracted all the time—it's much easier to be plugged in and entertained 24/7 than to be alone with ourselves. But of course that overstimulation is why we get stressed out and anxious and need meditation in the first place. Want to be more clear, more focused, more thoughtful, more aware, and more productive? Sit in silence for five minutes a day. You can do it! Check it off your list first thing in the morning with an app and your headphones (the Unplug app features guided meditations for everything from stressing less to eating healthier).

As you get more comfortable with it, you'll find that you're actually able to access that sense of calm and focus whenever things start to get too busy. When you practice first thing in the morning, before new distractions slide in, you're really building a skill that will serve you throughout the day.

DE-STRESS IN UNDER A MINUTE

1. Position both hands in front of your face as if you were giving 2 thumbs-up.
2. Turn your thumbs horizontally and place them on either side of the bridge of your nose, just beneath your brow bone.
3. Press firmly.
4. Count slowly for 8–10 seconds and breathe.
5. Reposition your thumbs slightly above the outside ends of each eyebrow.
6. Place your index fingers about an inch above your thumbs slightly toward each other.
7. Gently squeeze.
8. Count slowly for 8–10 seconds and breathe.
9. Carry on with whatever you were doing.

THE EXPERT:

Mehmet Oz, MD, is a professor of surgery at Columbia University, a bestselling author and the host of the Emmy-winning daytime talk show *The Dr. Oz Show.*

THE EXPLANATION:

Many people hold stress and tension in their head and face and, not to stress you out, but stress can damage every part of your body and lead to chronic disease. You'll definitely want to SEE PAGE 212 FOR TAKE A CALMING BREATH, PAGE 178 FOR HOW TO MEDITATE, and PAGE 242 FOR HOW TO LET SOMETHING GO but in the meantime, do a quick DIY head massage—a super-easy way to de-stress and reset your face. You can close your eyes if you're more comfortable, but you can also sneak this in in public or wherever you are whenever you need it. Just wash your hands before touching your face!

BREW A CUP OF TEA

1. Fill your teakettle with fresh, filtered water (resist the urge to just heat up what's sitting on the stove).

2. Bring the kettle to a boil. Green tea, white tea, and some oolongs require around 170°F water (that's considerably cooler than boiling, which is 212°F) so unless you're using an electric kettle with a thermometer, be sure you let the water cool before pouring.

3. If you're using loose-leaf tea (apparently we all should be), measure it out—it's usually 1 teaspoon per cup, but read the packaging. Put it into your teapot, or infuser. (Most teapots have either built-in infusers or a filter at the spout, which makes steeping both loose-leaf tea and tea bags really easy.)

4. Pour your water into the teapot and let it steep for 3–4 minutes (steeping time will depend on the specific tea you're using).

5. While you're waiting for the tea to steep in your pot, pour some of the boiling water from the kettle into your teacup to warm it (then dump it right before you pour in the tea).

6. If you're using a tea bag, put it in your cup, then pour the water over it. Let it steep for 2–4 minutes (don't dunk it up and down).

7. Remove the tea bag (don't squeeze it!) or the leaves/infuser from the cup before drinking.

THE EXPERT:

Tatjana Apukhtina is the founder of Teapro, a loose-tea subscription service based in London. Each month, subscribers receive a themed tea box containing teaware, unique tea varieties, and education about their history, benefits, and culture.

THE EXPLANATION:

Tea is mostly water, so the water you use *does* matter. Use filtered and always start fresh—anything previously boiled loses oxygen and can weaken the flavor of your tea. Some teas are very sensitive to high temperatures, while others need to be steeped with almost boiling water. As a rule of thumb, herbal teas need boiling water and a bit longer steeping time (about five minutes); green tea might get bitter if you use water that's too hot. When using loose-leaf tea, make sure your tea leaves have enough room to expand in whatever vessel you're brewing them in (Tatjana doesn't recommend using one of those mesh balls for infusing, as it constrains the tea; glass infusers or teapots with infusers built in yield the best flavor). And you can resteep the leaves you're using for most loose-leaf teas—at least three or four times. Some (particularly oolongs) even reveal new flavors as you resteep them. If you're using a tea bag, just let it sit in the cup and then remove it—don't dunk it and don't wring it out; when you squeeze out your bag, you're releasing the dregs where the tannins are most concentrated, which will make your tea bitter. (It can also be seen as a form of poor etiquette.) And don't add sugar to loose-leaf tea; it doesn't go well with good-quality tea and can even diminish the benefits. You'll also find you don't need it with loose-leaf tea; if you really have a sweet tooth, add some honey instead.

A word about tea bags:

Seek out tea bags where you can *see* the actual tea leaves—many paper tea bags contain dust, which is the lowest grade of tea (essentially leftovers). Also make sure the company you're using doesn't use plastic in their tea bags—some are made from materials that contain plastics which then dissolve into hot water, so you end up ingesting them. Um, good to know!

Bonus

More good-to-know tea facts:

- **Green tea:** Offers a high content of antioxidants (higher than black tea), which helps drain toxins from your body. It's good to drink at work when you want to improve long-term focus, while avoiding the jitters some people might get from coffee.
- **White tea:** L-theanine is an amino acid in tea that stimulates production of the relaxing neurotransmitter GABA, which has a calming effect on your mind. (White tea has the highest amount of L-theanine, which is why it's so relaxing.)
- **Chamomile:** Great tea to drink before going to bed. Chamomile tea relaxes your muscles and has a soothing effect on your nerves, helping you fall asleep naturally. It can also ease the headache and nausea that's often associated with a hangover.
- **Peppermint:** Peppermint has antispasmotic properties, which can calm the gut, minimizing cramps and preventing gas buildup. It is also known for reducing the feeling of nausea. Since peppermint tea is caffeine free, you can drink it any time in the day.
- **Matcha:** Matcha is a type of green tea made from powder (that comes from grinding the tea leaves) and contains the highest amount of antioxidants, which are good for your immunity and general well-being.

- **Black tea:** The most popular tea in the UK, it contains thearubigins and tannins that can help fight the flu and relieve its symptoms.

AVOID GETTING SICK

1. Eat garlic (raw is ideal—sorry, friends and family!—but cooked will help, too).
2. Drink immune-boosting tea; ginger and medicinal mushroom (yup, that's a thing!) are best.
3. Keep hand sanitizer accessible (on your desk or in your bag or in your car) but pay attention to the alcohol content; it must be at least 60 percent alcohol to be effective.
4. Use a saline spray in your nose before work.
5. Wash your hands after touching things (elevator buttons, door handles, that pen at the bank) and even *looking* at the guy who just sneezed.
6. Do an afternoon nasal spray. (Then wash your hands. Again.)

THE EXPERT:

Mehmet Oz, MD, is a professor of surgery at Columbia University, a bestselling author, and the host of the Emmy-winning daytime talk show *The Dr. Oz Show.*

THE EXPLANATION:

First you have to prep your body to fight the inevitable public space germs—at the office, on public transit, at the movie theater, etc.— then think about getting rid of the germs you've already caught. Eating garlic really boosts your immune system—it ups the production of your disease-fighting white blood cells—but that doesn't mean you have to chomp on a raw clove. Try mixing minced garlic into salad dressings or soups, making garlic toasts (mix minced garlic with butter or ghee, spread on a toasted baguette), add it to bean dips or, hello, tzatziki! Aim to incorporate a clove a day at least several times a week. The tea boosts energy and flushes toxins, and the saline works two ways: washing bacteria away before it can infect you, and preventing your nose from drying out (a dry nose makes it easier to get sick). And then hand-washing, as needed. And it's *always* needed—if we learned one thing during the coronavirus pandemic it's that we all touch our faces way more than we think. Hand sanitizer is good if it's all you have available, but it doesn't get rid of certain germs, like the norovirus, so be sure you're hand-washing, too. And you know you have to do that for twenty seconds, right?

Pro tip: Feel something coming on? Here's how to tell if it's a cold or the flu: Cold symptoms appear slowly over several days and affect your head (congestion, sneezing, sore throat) while the flu hits suddenly and affects your whole body (aches, fever, stomach troubles). Kinda makes you want to wash your hands again, amirite?

Bonus

When you use a public restroom, do you tend to skip the first stall and choose one farther away from the entrance? Yup! Experts theorize that people do this in order to have a little more privacy. But because the first stall is used least often, it contains the lowest bacteria levels. Amazing! Instead of skipping the first stall, choose it in order to help avoid possible infections.

TAKE A NAP

"The most important thing is to not overthink it, and get stressed
out by trying (and failing) to take the perfect nap. There are
several of our Thrive Microsteps, which are science-backed,
too-small-to-fail changes you can immediately incorporate
into your daily life, for getting better sleep that also apply
to taking a good nap."

—Arianna Huffington

1. Turn the room into a dark sleep sanctuary. Turn down the lights and draw the shades as soon as you start to get ready for sleep.

2. Rid the room of unwanted noise. Sound is one of the simplest and most direct impediments to sound sleep. Identify any sources of unwanted noise (starting with your devices) and either remove them from your room or silence them.

3. Keep the room cool (between 65 and 69 degrees). Set your thermostat to your preferred cool temperature. Research shows that even a small drop in body temperature sends a sleep signal to the brain to initiate sleep.

4. Use anything that helps you sleep. If you usually sleep with aids, like an eye mask and white noise, it's likely you'll be better able to nap when you give your body the sleep cues it normally gets.

5. Meditation can help—even a few deep breaths can quiet the mind and ease your transition into sleep. Sipping chamomile or lavender tea can also help calm your mind and shift you into sleep mode. You can change your perspective away from the worries of the day by jotting down a few things you're grateful for in a gratitude journal. A lot of people find this very effective at the end of the day before bed, but it has the same power during the day before a nap.

6. But most important is to get a nap as soon you realize you are running on empty, even if the conditions are not ideal. Experts

say that the best time to take a nap is when you're exhausted and you're able to.

THE EXPERT:

Arianna Huffington, founder and CEO of Thrive Global, the founder of *The Huffington Post*, and the author of fifteen books, including, most recently, *Thrive* and *The Sleep Revolution*. In 2016, she launched Thrive Global, a leading behavior-change tech company with the mission of changing the way we work and live by ending the collective delusion that burnout is the price we must pay for success.

THE EXPLANATION:

"While naps are not a substitute for getting adequate sleep at night, the science shows that naps boost our alertness, cognitive performance, and even our immune system. Naps are a great tool when you have not gotten adequate sleep the night before. If you have gotten adequate sleep, you don't need naps!" —Arianna Huffington

Pro tip: Taking a long nap can leave you with "sleep inertia," so if you need help waking up, setting an alarm is a good idea. But if you do, use an analog alarm clock so you can leave your phone charging in another room—that will help you wake up from the nap as recharged as your phone. The National Sleep Foundation recommends twenty to thirty minutes for a nap that will help you feel recharged without leaving you groggy.

BOOST YOUR ENERGY (IN THREE MINUTES)

1. Read through all the steps to get a sense of how this exercise works (it can be tricky at first).
2. Find a quiet, private place where you can sit down. Take a practice breath and feel your belly moving out as you inhale and contracting back as you breathe air out.
3. Set your phone timer for 1 minute and 30 seconds, then close your eyes.
4. Block your right nostril with your right thumb, breathe in through your left nostril.
5. Block your left nostril with your right ring finger, release your thumb, and blow the air out through your right nostril.
6. Repeat this action (inhaling through the left, exhaling through the right) as quickly as you can for 90 seconds. The breaths will be shallow.
7. When the timer goes off, drop your hand and inhale deeply through both nostrils. Then exhale completely.
8. Gently open your eyes and reset your timer for 1 minute and 30 seconds. Close your eyes again.
9. Block the left nostril with the right ring finger, breathe in through your right nostril.
10. Block the right nostril with your right thumb, release your ring finger, and exhale through the left nostril.
11. Now, begin to quicken your pace—inhale through the right, exhale through the left. Repeat for 90 seconds.
12. When the timer goes off, inhale fully through both nostrils and hold that breath for a moment. Then exhale completely and sit quietly for a moment with your eyes closed.
13. Notice the energy shift.

THE EXPERT:

Parvati Shallow is a professional adventurer, speaker, and internationally recognized yoga teacher (she holds advanced certifications in both Hatha and Kundalini Yoga) and three-time competitor of CBS's series *Survivor* (she won the whole thing in season 16).

THE EXPLANATION:

This rapid alternate nostril breathing is a practice that comes from the teachings of yoga. It's part of pranayama—breathing techniques that enliven vital energy—and it's great when you need a nice, smooth energy buzz without the jittery side effects of caffeine. Like, say, when 3 p.m. rolls around and everything in your world goes gray. Admittedly the exercise may seem a bit bizarre (hence finding a nice quiet place) and it can be awkward at first, so definitely start by practicing the techniques (you might also need a tissue—I know, I know). And, um, wash your hands before and after! There's a ton of incredible science behind pranayama, and these are powerful practices: If you feel light-headed or dizzy as you're fast-breathing, pause and take a few normal breaths. Return to the practice once you've regulated yourself. Gradually, you can build up to five minutes or more.

PAINT YOUR OWN NAILS

"The important thing to remember is that this takes a little bit of practice. Try not to get frustrated if the first time isn't perfect—if you mess up, you can clean it up!"

—Michelle Lee

1. Use the bathroom. (So you don't have to navigate this with wet nails—d'oh!)
2. Gather your base coat, polish, top coat, a nail file, an eye liner brush, and an acetone remover.

3. Find a large, flat, and stable surface to work on.

4. Remove any old polish, then file nails (file in only *one* direction to avoid creating jagged edges).

5. Wash your hands in warm, soapy water, but don't soak—soaking causes nails to expand, which can affect the painting process. Dry hands completely.

6. Before using each polish, slowly roll the bottle between your palms a few times; if it's separated, slowly turn upside down and back right side up but don't shake (shaking creates bubbles, which you don't want on your nails).

7. Place elbows *and* forearms on your flat surface and paint, resting the pinky-side edge of your painting hand on the table (this will stabilize your hand).

8. Apply base coat to one hand, then the other. Allow to dry for a minute or two. (Don't skip this step; you need a nice solid foundation.)

9. Take the polish brush out of the bottle, dripping excess into the bottle—you want to be left with *one* blob on *one* side of the brush.

10. Drop that blob in the center of your nail close to the cuticle but not right at the edge. Nudge the blob back toward the cuticle, then pull the brush forward to create a stripe down the center. Repeat on either side—you're aiming for three stripes—making sure to leave a little space between the sides of the nail and your cuticles.

11. Cap the edge of your nail with each coat by carefully swiping a small amount of polish along the edge of the nail (a pro trick that will help prevent chipping).

12. Repeat steps 9 through 11 on all nails, allowing the first hand to dry for a minute or two before switching.

13. Once the first coat has partially dried (a minute or two depending on the polish), apply a second coat in the same way.

14. Fix any mistakes using a stiff-bristled makeup brush (like an eyeliner brush), dipped in acetone.

15. Apply the top coat to both hands and allow nails to dry completely (drying drops or a fan will help speed things along).

THE EXPERT:

Michelle Lee is the editor in chief of *Allure*, the first and only dedicated beauty magazine. In 2017, *Adweek* named *Allure* "Magazine of the Year" and Michelle "Editor of the Year." Michelle is a huge nail art fan, and she posts her tutorials and stunning creations on Instagram with the hashtag #michelleleenails.

THE EXPLANATION:

You don't have to give yourself a full manicure, but at least remove any polish and wash your hands. (If you're getting a professional manicure about once a month, doing your own in between is even easier.) DO NOT put on hand lotion before painting; you need a clean, dry surface for the polish to last. You can push cuticles back during the hand-washing step using the thumbnail of the opposite hand to nudge them back—and trim any hangnails with nail clippers or cuticle scissors. If you can, paint your nails in the *morning.* Polish is not fully dry for a couple of hours, and you tend to be less careful of your nails in the evening (and your bed is wet nails' enemy). Michelle paints her nondominant hand first because seeing that one done well gives her a boost of confidence to tackle the other one. One trick for painting *with* your nondominant hand: Hold the polish brush still over the nail and move your dominant hand under it (as opposed to moving the brush hand, which may be shaky). And paint a relatively thin coat—if it's too thick they're not going to dry and you'll get smudges (thinner polishes will dry faster; older, thicker polishes will take a little longer).

Pro tip: The number one way to extend the life of a manicure: Don't use your nails as tools! Don't use them to peel the sticker labels off things or to pop a seltzer can, and never go digging into the bottom of your bag for things without being really mindful. Refresh your top coat a few days after you paint, and apply moisturizer and lotion to your hands throughout the week.

PREPARE FOR A WORKOUT (SO YOU ACTUALLY WORK OUT)

"The best workout you can do is the one that you will stick with."
—Liz Plosser

1. Say "I *get* to work out" not "I *have* to work out." (i.e., reframe how you talk and think about your workouts).
2. Make it nonnegotiable. Don't say "I'd like to get to the gym tomorrow" or "I'm gonna try to go out for a run"; tell yourself you're doing it, schedule time for it on your calendar, and make it happen.
3. Lay your clothes out the night before (or pack your gym bag and leave it by the door).
4. Check the weather and plan accordingly. Obviously important for outdoor workouts, but even if you're driving to a class, the right gear makes a huge difference in how enjoyable the whole experience will be.
5. Have a specific plan. On days when your mind is just not in it, make it easier on yourself by knowing exactly what you're going to do before you start (i.e., don't just show up at the gym and wander around aimlessly).
6. Use music to get your energy up—or down. Start listening to your pump-up playlist (or mellow yoga jams) a few minutes *before* your workout.
7. Eat a 100- to 300-calorie snack (a combo of carbs and protein works well, which is why nutrition bars are a good go-to). This will be different for everyone, and based on the time of day you're working out, but something to fuel you is important; experiment to see what works for you.
8. Don't waste time with workouts you find yourself dreading—just because your friends are training for their first half marathon or say they've never felt better now that they've picked

up _____ [insert latest fitness trend] doesn't mean it will be right for you.

9. Follow only the fitness people on social media who lift you up (and *unfollow* any who make you feel bad about yourself or just kind of annoy you). It's your time, it's your motivation, it's your inspiration—curate it carefully.

10. Remind yourself that future you will be so grateful you did this. No one ever says, "Oh, man, I wish I hadn't just worked out."

THE EXPERT:

Liz Plosser is the editor in chief of *Women's Health*, the global health and wellness authority, with twenty-nine editions in fifty-three countries. Prior to *WH*, Liz was director of content and communications at SoulCycle. She's run ten marathons, at least a hundred half marathons (not a typo, folks!), and completed a Half Ironman. She also has her personal training certification.

THE EXPLANATION:

Next time you're sick or injured (or, um, quarantined) and can't even get out for a walk, remember how badly you crave movement. Working out is a luxury and it's easy to forget that, especially if you're rifling through your drawers for leggings in the pitch dark at 6 a.m. like a raccoon digging through the trash (Liz has been there). Mind-set—and laying out your clothes!—is important. That said, don't rely on mind-set for everything because there will be days when your mind is working against you; *that's* when the nonnegotiable trick kicks in. Some days you have to muscle through, and having a preplanned workout helps—if your brain is already using a lot of energy just to motivate you, have those decisions premade. Am I doing the rower? Do I do intervals? Should I take a spin class? There are countless ways to have other people figure this out for you (a trainer on Instagram, a fitness app, a class you sign up for in advance). Another way to ease your decision-making: Stick with the clothes that work for your body. New gear is fun, but at the end of the day there are only a few leggings and sneakers and tops that we all reach for over and over. Find what they are and keep buying them.

Pro tip: When you're getting ready for a workout, think of yourself like a toddler who's heading out for the day. When moms are dealing with little kids they make sure they have their snack, and their water, that they're dressed warmly (but not too warm!), and that they've gone...potty. If you're going to invest the time in going for a workout, you should take the (baby) steps to set yourself up for success. And you're much more likely to do it again the next day if you've been kind to yourself!

Bonus

Don't have time for a "real" workout? Magazine editors have been saying it for decades, but that's because it's true. Find ways to work in extra steps throughout your day. Take the stairs, park farther away at the store, do a work call while walking around the block, get up and go to someone's desk when you need to debrief after a meeting. And there is no shortage of quick, virtual workouts for nonideal circumstances floating around these days that you can pull up on your phone.

STRETCH AFTER A WORKOUT

"Working out without stretching is like ending a sentence without punctuation."

—Amanda Kloots

Hold each of these stretches for just a couple of breaths (if you need more time in a certain place, take it; stretching is different for everyone).

1. Lying flat on your back with your feet outstretched, bring your right knee to your chest and hug it tight.
2. Extend the right leg to the ceiling, holding the back of your thigh with both hands and pulling it toward your chest until you feel a deep stretch in your hamstring. (You can loop a towel around the bottom of your foot and use the ends to pull your leg toward you, which will help keep your neck and back on the ground.)
3. Bend your left leg with your foot flat on the ground and cross your right ankle over your left knee. Reach through the hole with your right hand and interlace your hands behind your left knee. Pull your left leg toward you for an outer thigh and glute stretch.
4. Put both feet down flat by your butt with your knees bent, and let your right knee fall open to the floor. Pull it back up and repeat a few times to open up your hip.
5. Stretch your left leg out straight, stretch your arms out to make a T, then cross your right knee over the left side of your body. Look in the opposite direction (this is a yoga twist and it helps wring out waste—so good for your insides).
6. Repeat steps 1–5 with the opposite leg.
7. Sit up and stretch both legs out in a straddle position.
8. Stretch your arms high over your head, then over to your right foot for a few counts (you should feel this in your oblique muscles), then to your left foot, and then forward for an inner-thigh stretch.

9. Stand up and place your right arm across your body, using your left arm to hold it in place. Tilt your head in the opposite direction to get a neck stretch, then point your right elbow to the ceiling with your palm flat on your back for a tricep stretch. Use your left hand to push the elbow back for an added stretch.

10. Shake out your arms and repeat with your left.

11. Lace your fingers behind your back and push them down toward the floor, while reaching up to the ceiling with your chin (this is an opposition stretch and feels really good any time of day).

12. Come up on the balls of your feet to stretch out your arches and your feet.

13. Fold your body in half, hanging your head toward the floor, and grab opposite elbows in your hands. Slowly swing from left to right. Release your arms and shake your head yes and no.

14. Slowly roll up, one vertebrae at a time, thinking about stacking your body as you go—knees on top of ankles, hips on top of knees, shoulders on top of hips. Your head comes up last.

15. End with a power pose. Widen your stance, and stretch your arms out so your body makes an X. Open your chest up toward the ceiling and lift up your head.

THE EXPERT:

Amanda Kloots is a former Broadway dancer, former Radio City Rockette, and current celebrity trainer. She developed the wildly popular AK! Rope method of working out with just a jump rope for a quick, effective way to get a full body workout.

THE EXPLANATION:

The point of stretching is to prevent injury, but also to calm your body down. Take deep breaths throughout to lower your heart rate and bring oxygen into those muscles, which will help with any lactic acid buildup. In other words, DON'T SKIP THE POST-WORKOUT STRETCH. It's really important and will only take about five minutes, though the more you stretch the better (adding a stretch session like this before bed is a great way to wind down and bring on good sleep). Finish with your head hanging between your legs; this releases the tension built up in your back and neck throughout the workout and can set you up with great posture for the day. And the power pose just reminds you to make yourself as big as you can and open yourself up to every possibility. Boom!

Bonus

Not in a place where you can lay on the floor? Get your hamstrings by standing with your feet together, bending your knees and placing your hands flat on the floor. Take a deep breath and try to straighten your knees as much as you can, then exhale and bend again. Repeat a few times. (It's a Rockette stretch!) Standing straight again, pull each ankle to your butt with your hand for a quad stretch, then place one foot at a time against a wall and hug your body toward the wall to hit your calves. Widen your stance and reach down to touch your toes with the opposite hand for a modified twist.

SAY NO (TO SOMETHING YOU FEEL LIKE YOU SHOULD SAY YES TO BUT DON'T REALLY WANT TO)

"The question isn't would I rather do this thing or nothing, it's would I rather do this thing or everything else in my already packed life that I'm currently living."

—Laura Vanderkam

1. Remind yourself that time is valuable and once it's spent you absolutely can't get it back.
2. Ask yourself this: "Would I be willing to do this thing *tomorrow*?" (It's easy to sign yourself up for something in April when

it's only September. Do your future self a favor and try this little exercise.)

3. Respond quickly—don't leave people hanging once you know you're saying no.

4. Instead of saying you don't have time, try this: "Thanks so much for thinking of me, I'm not going to be able to take this on but I wish you the best with X." (If it's not a priority because something else actively is, own it and be OK with it.)

5. Reframe your "no" to assuage guilt. This is so important that it deserves someone's full energy, and since I can't do that because I have XYZ other thing, I would be dishonoring the importance of this event/role/weekend getaway by saying yes.

THE EXPERT:

Laura Vanderkam is a time-management expert and author of several books including *Off the Clock: Feel Less Busy While Getting More Done, What the Most Successful People Do Before Breakfast*, and *168 Hours: You Have More Time Than You Think*. Her TED Talk "How to Gain Control of Your Free Time" has been viewed more than 8 million times.

THE EXPLANATION:

Having a sense of time's value reminds you that saying no to something now will allow you to say yes to something else later. You want to be sure you're saying no to the things you don't really want to be doing, the things that are not particularly aligned with your goals, or activities that are not meaningful or enjoyable to you or to the people you care about. Clear your calendar and energy to say yes to the big stuff, the meaningful, the exciting, and potentially scary but boundary-pushing stuff that would actually be enriching to take on. It's very easy to disregard our future self, whom we often view as a different person from our present self. Either we think, *Oh, she's going to be incredibly productive so this will be fine for her to take on* or we think, *Oh, that's* her *problem—whatever I sign her up for is* hers *to deal with.*

"Would I say yes tomorrow?" is a helpful way to consider things. Because you know exactly how much energy you'll have tomorrow, exactly what you'll have on your plate tomorrow, exactly what the opportunity cost is for tomorrow. If you'd be willing to move stuff around or miss things to say yes to this invite *tomorrow*, then you'll likely be happy to do it whenever it comes. If not, there's your answer. Which you should *not* leave open-ended. (If you say, "I can't do this thing because I'm busy then," you're leaving it open for them to find another date to work around your schedule.)

Bonus

If that thing you feel like you should do involves people you like spending time with, consider this: People, in general, are a good use of time (and, let's face it, being able to get together is not always a guarantee). Yes, it takes effort to get there, but you'll probably be happier looking back on it if you spent your evening going out to dinner with friends rather than scrolling through Instagram looking at other people's dinner parties. You want to have a good amount of effort-*full* fun in your life and not just the effortless kind. Ask: "Will my future self be glad I did this?" Sometimes that can nudge us to do the things we would enjoy that might take a little extra effort (like getting in the car when it's raining out or putting on pants).

··· 12 ···

UP YOUR PERSONAL GAME

WALK INTO A ROOM WITH CONFIDENCE

1. Come up with an opening line to use when you get where you're going.
2. Check yourself out in a mirror (or your phone); make adjustments as needed.
3. Take a deep breath.
4. Notice the adrenaline flooding your body and focus on using it to energize you.
5. Say "I've got this" out loud. A little embarrassing but...you've got this.
6. Stand tall, smile, and go.

THE EXPERT:

Lydia Fenet is the country's leading benefit auctioneer, managing director at Christie's, and author of *The Most Powerful Woman in the Room Is You.*

THE EXPLANATION:

Knowing exactly what you're going to say once you get into a room—even if it's a simple "Anyone else get caught in that rain out there?"—squashes nerves because you're not leaving things to chance (or awkward silences). And making sure you've got nothing in your teeth means you won't be fidgeting or obsessing as you walk. The deep breath creates a pause and allows you to use the ice water running through your veins as fuel for whatever you're heading into—even if it's just a regular work meeting. Chances are you are your own worst critic, so giving yourself the "You've got this" pep talk is the perfect final step before checking your posture and heading in. Remember, confidence is infectious!

MAKE MORE MINDFUL DECISIONS

"Mindfulness is a buzzy concept these days but it's really just the practice of being aware of what you're doing when you're doing it. Mindfulness changes the way you see, hear, touch, smell, and taste. It will change the way you interact with people. It will change your mood and productivity—it's the most readily available game changer there is!"

—Nicole Lapin

1. Before making a decision (or when you notice that you're mind *full* instead of mindful), stop and take a beat.
2. Breathe. FOR A 16-SECOND CALMING BREATH, SEE PAGE 212.
3. Tap into your senses with the 5-4-3-2-1 Method: Notice five things you see, four things you can touch, three things you can hear, two things you can smell, and one thing you can taste.
4. Get up and walk around if you need to further regroup.
5. Process the situation. What is *actually* happening—not in your head but in reality?
6. Name any emotions you're feeling. (Forcing yourself to articulate exactly what you're feeling can actually reduce that emotion.)

7. Now that you know what's happening, determine the best thing to do in response.
8. Do it.

THE EXPERT:

Nicole Lapin is the author of *Becoming Super Woman: A Simple 12-Step Plan to Go from Burnout to Balance.* She was the youngest-ever anchor on CNN before holding the same title at CNBC, anchoring the network's early-morning show while covering business topics for MSNBC and *Today.* She's also the author of *Rich Bitch* and *Boss Bitch.*

THE EXPLANATION:

Most people forget to be mindful the moment they hop out of bed and especially when they step into work mode. Mindfulness techniques (like the 5-4-3-2-1 Method) help you to slow down and act more intentionally in the face of constant distraction (as does putting down your damn phone—for TIPS ON HOW TO UNPLUG SEE PAGE 240). But the general idea here is to pause, process, then pounce.[3] When you're more aware, you can make informed choices that are in accordance with your values. Nicole's three *P* words are simple (and the cute alliteration will make it easier to remember), but pausing is a skill that takes practice. Every decision we make is made up of thousands of other baby decisions. Before making those decisions, whether with your mind or your gut, you have to take a beat. Research shows that pausing for fifty to one hundred milliseconds helps the brain focus on the information relevant for the decision while blocking out distractions. Sometimes the decision (soup or salad?) doesn't matter, so neither does the pause. But the

---

3. Post the three Ps—pause, process, pounce—on your computer screen to remind you to take a beat before firing off an angry email.

more important the decision, the more important that pause—and being present—becomes. Learn to *be*, first and foremost, and the *doing* will come.

Pro tip: When you're hungry, angry, lonely, or tired (or HALT), you're most likely to make poor decisions. Don't let these negative stressors trigger the wrong choice. If you're HALT, then *halt* decision-making until you're not.

A Harvard Study found that we pay attention to what we're doing only 47 percent of the time. Meaning more than half of our time is spent not even paying attention to what we're supposed to be paying attention to! **How mindful are you? Ask yourself these questions:**

Does your mind tend to wander during conversations that last more than ten seconds?

Do you spend conversations thinking about what you're going to say next instead of listening to what's being said now?

Do you check your phone during conversations, use it during meetings, and keep it on the table during meals?

Do you get from one place to another and realize you have no memory of the walk or drive you just took?

Do you have trouble taking one task to completion before wandering off to start something new?

Do you frequently make impulsive decisions or blurt out whatever comes to mind?

Do you get so overwhelmed by your jumble of thoughts or feelings that you feel paralyzed and unable to make decisions or articulate opinions?

The more yes answers you have, the more of a problem you have staying present. But mindfulness is a skill—you can and will get better at it!

SET GOALS

"I'm a big believer in first figuring out where you want to go in life and then reverse engineering how you're going to get there."

—Nicole Lapin

1. Define for yourself what "it all" means to you (keep in mind that this is going to look different for everyone), and acknowledge that "having it all" and "doing it all" are not the same thing.

2. Write down your finance goals. (You probably have some general goals for how you want your career and earning power to progress in your head, but have you actually spelled out what they are? In order to hold yourself accountable, clear metrics are important.)

3. List your family goals. It doesn't matter whether you want to have 10 kids or 10 cats, the point of this exercise is to outline what "having it all" looks like for *you*.

4. Come up with fun goals (vacations you want to take, new activities you want to try, perhaps a beach condo to buy someday—yes, these are important to include!).

5. Create fitness goals. (This doesn't mean "I want sick abs," it means thinking about what you want your body to be able to do. Run a marathon? Play sports with your kids? Carry 5 bags of groceries to your 4th-floor walk-up apartment without getting winded? And taking care of your mind and soul, too.)

6. For each of the four categories from above, sort goals into the following:
   - one-year goals
   - three-year goals
   - five-year goals
   - seven-year goals
   - ten-year goals

7. Look back to see if your career choices cover what you want to achieve in the other areas of your life (i.e., are you going to make enough money to afford that beach house in 10 years).

8. Make sure the choices you make about how you spend your day are bringing you closer to your goals—make different choices as needed.

9. Readjust your goals as often as needed; just be sure to create a corresponding plan to get where you want to go.

10. If you start to feel envious of what others have, go back and look at your goal list. Is it on yours now? Nope? Then that's not what "having it all" looks like for you at this point in your story.

THE EXPERT:

Nicole Lapin is the author of *Becoming Super Woman: A Simple 12-Step Plan to Go from Burnout to Balance.* She was the youngest-ever anchor on CNN before holding the same title at CNBC, anchoring the network's early-morning show, while covering business topics for MSNBC and *Today.* She's also the author of *Rich Bitch* and *Boss Bitch.*

THE EXPLANATION:

To achieve success you have to set yourself up for it, which means first figuring out what "it" is. How do you have it all? You decide what "having it all" means to you in all four *F* categories (Finance, Family, Fun, Fitness) and then come up with an action plan to have *that.* Breaking the goals into shorter time lines is good because "What do I want to be doing in ten years?" can be a very daunting question. Those smaller, more manageable pieces make planning the future feel far less overwhelming and much more doable. And don't forget to add some mental health and emotional wellness goals to your fitness section. Realistically, the money from your career should power the rest of your goals, so as you flesh out the rest of the *F*s, check back and see if your career goals will get you where you want to be. It's cool to have actual money numbers as goals (a targeted salary or bonus, for example), but it's more constructive to determine what you would do with that money. Fun is fun, but it can also be expensive and time-consuming (and so can kids), so in step one really think about what kind of life you want. Do you want to take quarterly vacations? Monthly girls' weekends? Weekly date nights? Decide that first, then figure out what the dollar figure is to live that life.

Fun fact: A major study on goal setting found that only 3 percent of people set clear intentions and actually wrote their goals down. But on average those people earned ten times as much money as the other 97 percent. (Excuse me while I go write down my goals.)

STOP OBSESSING ABOUT SOMETHING BAD THAT MAY OR MAY NOT HAPPEN

1. Think about the worst things that could happen based on this information.
2. Let your mind go completely down the what-if rabbit hole for a minute or two. What would *really* happen if the worst thing happens?
3. Come up with a plan of action for each potential shit-storm you envisioned—what would you *actually* do if you got, say, fired or dumped or *cancer*? Think it through. Verbalize it to a friend or loved one if you like.
4. Write down those solutions (*OK, so you get fired, now you do X, Y, Z*). Jot it down on a piece of paper or make a very clear mental note.
5. File that plan away—either in a mental box or that shoebox you keep tripping over in your closet.

6. Next time the what-if creeps into your mind (because it will), remind yourself that you already have a plan for that, so there's no need to obsess. Thank you, next!

THE EXPERT:

Ethan Zohn is a motivational speaker, two-time cancer survivor, winner of CBS's *Survivor: Africa*, and a former professional soccer player. He and his wife, Lisa, would use this technique when he was battling cancer *and* while he was playing *Survivor: Winners at War* in 2020. She actually taught it to Ethan. (Thanks, Lisa!)

THE EXPLANATION:

We all worry about the what-if scenario. It's there and we can't ignore it, so we *shouldn't*. Instead of trying to stop ourselves from going there, *go* there. All the way. (That said, if you get stuck in the rabbit hole for too long, stop yourself—stand up, take a few breaths, clap loudly, whatever you need to get yourself out of your head.) The most important step: Your game plan and how you press on. Then *move* on. If you—and your brain—know that you have a plan of attack should you need it, you won't need to obsess over and over about something that may or may not happen.

Bonus

Is your mind in a particularly bad patch of what-ifs? Wear a rubber band around your wrist. Every time a negative thought creeps in, snap the band to quickly interrupt the negative thought pattern. Then pull up a good memory from your own memory bank—it could be finishing that 10K last summer, having a baby, graduating from college, *anything* that made you feel great. Replace the bad thought with the good thought, and allow yourself to really feel the positive vibes from that moment. This takes practice, but after a while the time between a bad thought and a good thought will become milliseconds. You're essentially retraining your brain not to go negative.

DO A QUICK GUT CHECK OF YOUR SPENDING

"If your leg broke you would never berate yourself for not knowing how to set your own bone. Are you a medical doctor? When it comes to money we think that by nature of us getting older we should somehow know how to manage our money. Did you go to money management school? No? Then you need help with this stuff."
—Tiffany Aliche, aka "the Budgetnista"

1. Create a monthly money list of all the places your money goes. Include *everything* you spend on from bills to hair to oat milk lattes.
2. Next to each of the items on your money list, write down how much you spend on that *monthly* (estimate if necessary).
3. Divide quarterly/annual expenses—if your water bill is $90 due every three months, list it as $30 in step 2. (If you get your nails done every two weeks and it's $40, list that as $80 in step 2.)
4. Add up all expenses on your money list. This is typically the "tears and tissues" step. *Wait a minute, I spend how much?!*
5. Write down your monthly *take-home* pay. Not your monthly salary, but the amount you actually get to put into your account.
6. Subtract what you spend a month from what you take home a month (step 5 minus step 4).
7. Take out a recent credit or debit card statement and glance over your purchases. Are they generally aligned with who you are and who/where you want to be in your life?

THE EXPERT:

Tiffany Aliche, aka "the Budgetnista," is a financial educator and author of *The One Week Budget* and *Live Richer Challenge*. In 2019 she wrote and helped pass "the Budgetnista Law," which makes it mandatory for financial education to be integrated into all middle schools in New Jersey.

THE EXPLANATION:

If you go to the doctor because you don't feel well they're not going to hand you heart medication; they're going to do a thorough workup. That's what this is: your checkup. The specific time frame of a month is the best way to get a clear picture of money in/money out. The reason steps 1 and 2 are separate is so you don't forget anything. When people just write down all their expenses we tend to leave out things, like restaurants or grooming, because we think of that spending as inconsequential. But when you write down *just* the word (takeout, nails, gas) without any amounts attached, you tend to include more things. Don't know where your money goes? Your debit and credit cards do, so pull out your latest statement. Once you've done the subtracting, are you negative? Are you positive? Don't panic—this is just the assessment. Most people are negative. Or they're slightly positive but have no idea where that extra money is (hint: It gets frittered away on stuff you're not accounting for). But if you don't recognize the person in step 7, it might be time to make some changes—and a budget. FOR ONE WAY TO SPEND LESS, SEE PAGE 85.

USE PROPER GRAMMAR (BECAUSE THIS STUFF AIN'T EASY)

1. Know the difference between **you're and your**: *Your* is the possessive of *you*, and *you're* is a contraction of *you are*. If you are not sure which one to use, try adding *you are* to the sentence to see if it still makes sense. For example: "You are really smart" means the same thing as "You're really smart"; "You are gold star" does not mean the same thing as "Your gold star." Two totally different words!

2. And ***their/they're/there***: *Their* is the possessive of *they*, and *they're* is a contraction of *they are*. *There* is a location (or a pro-noun to introduce a clause or a word—"There is an important lesson on this page"). Three totally different words! If you write *they're*, be sure you can replace it with *they are*: "They are arriving at noon" works, but "My parents are bringing they are dog" and "Put Bodie's pet food over they are" don't work.

3. And ***passed/past***: *Passed* is the past tense of the verb *to pass*. *Past* refers to a previous time. "In the past, my car was so slow that scooters passed me."

4. ***Further/farther***: In American English, *farther* is for physical distance (note that *farther* has the word *far* in it), and *further* is for metaphorical distance (e.g., "Don't bother me further"). *Further* is used more liberally in British English.

5. ***Affect/effect***: Although there are exceptions, most of the time *affect* is a verb, and *effect* is a noun. "The sound effects affected the ravens in the park." A trick to remember the two words' common roles is to think of the word *RAVEN*, which has the letters *A*, *V*, *E*, and *N*, which stand for "*affect* verb *effect* noun."

6. ***Then/than***: *Then* has a sense of time, and *than* is used to make a comparison. "Squiggly realized he had less ice cream than Aardvark. Then he threw a fit."

7. ***Lay/lie***: If you just focus on the setting/reclining meaning of *lay* and *lie*, then the important distinction is that *lay* requires a direct object, and *lie* does not. You lie on the sofa (no direct object), but you lay the book on the table (the book is the direct object). One theory is that people confuse *lay* and *lie* because of the children's prayer that reads "Now I lay me down to sleep." The archaic phrasing of the prayer is confusing, but remember: In that example, you are actually laying yourself down, just as you'd lay a book on the table. You use *lay* because it has an object—it's just an odd object.

THE EXPERT:

Mignon Fogarty, aka "Grammar Girl," is the founder of the Quick and Dirty Tips network (and podcast) and author of seven books on language, including the *New York Times* bestseller *Grammar Girl's Quick and Dirty Tips for Better Writing*. She's an inductee into the Podcasting Hall of Fame and a five-time winner of Best Education Podcast in the Podcast Awards.

THE EXPLANATION:

If you have trouble remembering these confusing words, it often helps to memorize single sentences that use each of them properly. Then, if you get tripped up, you can compare your new sentence to the one you've memorized and that you know is right. And while you're at it, it's "all of a sudden," not "all of *the* sudden"; it's "supposedly," not "supposably" (if what you're meaning to convey is that something is assumed to be true), and it's "could *not* care less," not "could care less" (although that last one is becoming more and more acceptable, just to keep us utterly confused!).

Bonus

Use *me*, *myself*, and *I* properly. Many people avoid using *me* because when we were kids and said things like "Me and Brooke are going to 7/11," it was hammered into us to stop saying "me" all the time (or was that just...me?). Use *me* when it's the object pronoun (the person or things having something done to them): "Send the email to Jose and me." (The thing being *done* to you is someone sending the email.) Use *I* when it's the subject pronoun (the person or things doing something): "Jose and I are looking forward to reading your email." (The thing you're *doing* is looking forward.) To make sure you have it right you can take the other person out of the sentence to see if it still makes sense: So for "Send the email to Jose and me," you'd think to yourself, "Send the email to [Jose and] me," and then it works. (If you'd said, "Send the email to Jose and I," it wouldn't work because when you remove Jose it becomes "Send the email to I," and that's just wrong.) Always put yourself last in lists of people, whether you're using *me* or *I*. This is more about politeness than grammar. Finally, use *myself* only after you have already referred to yourself in the sentence (e.g., "I baked the cake myself") or when you want to add emphasis ("I myself witnessed the murder").

CALM DOWN BEFORE REACTING

1. Think about the thing that's causing you anxiety.
2. Now, close your eyes and slowly inhale to the count of four as you visualize your breath.
3. Keep watching that breath go down into your belly; when it gets there hold it to the count of four.
4. Now, exhale and watch your breath as it flows back up and out to the count of four.
5. Hold the exhale for four seconds.
6. Open your eyes and breathe normally.
7. Ask yourself: "Were you thinking about that stressful thing when you were counting and breathing?" Exactly.
8. Repeat as needed.

THE EXPERT:

davidji is an internationally recognized stress-management expert, meditation teacher, and the author of *destressifying: The Real-World Guide to Personal Empowerment, Lasting Fulfillment, and Peace of Mind* (he teaches the sixteen-second breath to marines and calls it "tactical breathing").

THE EXPLANATION:

This breathing exercise is about interrupting the pattern to reset your brain. Taking a long deep breath and observing it go deep down into your belly and then watching it slowly coming back out creates the space we need. You can't think about what's stressing you because you're thinking about your breath (or trying not to pass out? just me?). When you get to the seventeenth second, sure, there's a chance you go right back into that original mind-set, but there's a higher likelihood that you're going to react differently because of that simple break in the action. Try this technique before answering a frustrating text or as you wait thirty-two minutes for customer service to pick up. You can even do it while sitting in traffic—or at a family dinner table—just don't close your eyes. Practice so it becomes a tool you can call on any time. (Do it four times in a row and you're meditating!)

Bonus

Thinking (or in this case breathing) before reacting is always a good idea. As Albert Einstein said, "Energy cannot be created or destroyed; it can only be changed from one form to another." This means if you react and say something you shouldn't have, or left someone feeling like crap, you can't take it back. And that negative energy has a ripple effect through their day and yours. Before you interact with anyone, try thinking about what kind of energy you're going to leave behind—is it positive or is it negative? davidji teaches about leaving either "Ojas" (sweet vital emotional nectar) or "Ama" (toxic residue). Sweet vital nectar for me, please!

GET YOURSELF THROUGH A TOUGH TIME

"Remember that you have survived every terrible day, every hard thing, every awful circumstance, and every heartbreak you've ever felt. You did whatever it took to deliver yourself here, and no matter how you feel about where you're at right now, or where you'd like to go from here, the making-it-here is an achievement worth honoring."
—Emily McDowell

1. Think of yourself as a caterpillar transforming into a butterfly—when you're in a cocoon you're fumbling and flailing around in the darkness, breaking shit, bumping up against unfamiliar edges: This is all necessary and on purpose.

2. Remind yourself: There is no such thing as failure. There is only learning. (Sometimes we end up learning what *not* to do, and that's OK.)

3. Look for happiness in the right direction (things that actually make us happy: time in nature, play, sleep, rest, nutrition, connection, love, touch, and movement).

4. Remember that it's impossible to hate yourself into feeling good. The defense mechanism of "If I'm cruel to myself first, it will hurt less if others are cruel to me later" is a flawed theory.

5. Try not to say anything to yourself that you wouldn't say to your best friend. Our inner voices and critics tell ourselves all sorts of nasty things we'd never dream of saying to anyone else.

6. Don't look back and beat yourself up. In hindsight, it's easy to look back on past choices and think "WTF was I thinking?" but whatever you were thinking made sense to you at the time.

THE EXPERT:

Emily McDowell is the creative director and founder of the greeting card company Emily McDowell & Friends. They make products that speak to the human condition with humor, and heart.

Emily is a writer and illustrator, and the author of *There Is No Good Card for This: What to Say and Do When Life Gets Scary, Awful, and Unfair to People You Love.*

THE EXPLANATION:

It's all about mind-set here—and being patient with yourself: When we're in the process of transformation, when everything feels dark and murky and pointless: This is the cocoon. And from the inside, it's almost impossible to see your time line, and to know when you're *this close* to coming out the other side. Because being in it feels only like being surrounded by darkness until, suddenly, you're not. And surprise: You can fly. You've heard it before but it bears repeating: When things don't go the way you'd hoped, remember that sometimes what seems like a terrible failure will turn out to be the best thing that ever happened to you. We may end up learning about ourselves, or others, or both. And when you're feeling sad or disengaged and you want to do something about it, get in touch with your essential, basic nature. Focus on the things that, biologically, make you happy.

Bonus

Want to put some good energy out there? If you love someone, tell them—and tell them WHY. Don't just say "I love you"—tell them, specifically, the things you think are so special about them. Texting is great for this. And if you do know someone is struggling, let them know you see them in what they're going through, and remind them that they're doing a good job.

Pro tip: Be nice to yourself. "The longer I'm alive, the more I believe that being kind to ourselves is absolutely our most important job here." —Emily McDowell

RESOLVE TO DO SOMETHING AND FOLLOW THROUGH

"Resolutions—made right—can make a huge difference in boosting happiness."

—Gretchen Rubin

1. Ask yourself: "What would make me happier?" It might be having more of *something good* (fun with friends, time for a hobby) or having less of *something bad* (yelling at your kids, regretting what you've eaten) or fixing something that doesn't feel right.
2. Identify a concrete habit that would bring about that change. Think specific and actionable. Instead of "find more joy in life" think "watch a classic movie every Sunday night."
3. Think about whether you're a "yes" resolver or a "no" resolver (i.e., do you want to resolve TO do something or NOT to do something?) and frame your resolution to reflect that (either don't do X or *do* do Y).
4. Ask yourself: "Am I starting small enough? Or big enough?" Push yourself too hard and you may screech to a halt. Or you may need to go big if you're someone who loses interest or gets discouraged by taking things slow and steady.
5. Come up with a plan to hold yourself accountable. (If you're an obliger, remember that external accountability is *key* for you, so find some friends to check in with.)

THE EXPERT:

Gretchen Rubin is the author of *The Happiness Project*, *Happier at Home*, *Better Than Before*, *The Four Tendencies*, and *Outer Order, Inner Calm*. She's the host of the award-winning podcast *Happier with Gretchen Rubin*, where she shares insights, strategies, and stories to help people understand themselves and create a happier life.

THE EXPLANATION:

The secret to success here is knowing your own nature. Start thinking about what would make the next week, month, and year happier for you (the more your life reflects your values, the happier you'll be; habits help ensure your life reflects your values). One common problem is that people make abstract resolutions. "Enjoy the now" is difficult to measure and therefore difficult to keep. Instead, look for a specific, measurable action that will carry you toward that abstract goal like "drink my coffee on my front steps every morning." When it comes to making permanent life changes, people tend to fall into one of two camps: Some people need to set small, consistent goals for themselves on a path to larger change (I'll go for a ten-minute walk at lunch every day); other people need the energy and excitement of a sweeping change in order to create a new habit (I'm waking up an hour early every day to go to the gym before work!). Both approaches work, so think about what works best for you and calibrate your goals accordingly. Finally, accountability is the secret to sticking to resolutions. Create one of Gretchen's "Better Than Before" habits groups with friends, or set goals and review dates for yourself on your calendar. That's the reason why step 2 is so important—if your resolution is too vague, it's hard to be held accountable (a resolution to "eat healthier" is harder to track than "eat salad for lunch three times a week").

Bonus

Need a good new habit to stick to? Try the one-minute rule: You must do any task that can be finished in one minute rather than putting it off till later. Hang up your coat, read a letter and toss it, fill in a form, put a dish in the dishwasher, etc. Because the tasks are so quick, it isn't too hard to make yourself follow the rule—but it has big results. Keeping all those small, nagging tasks under control will make you less overwhelmed; your home will probably be tidier and your productivity greater, too (you'll get so many little things done quickly, you'll have more time for the bigger tasks). As Gretchen says, it's an incredibly easy, incredibly effective way to boost happiness—but it must be followed consistently if you want to see results.

Pro tip: Rather than just focusing on to-do lists, make a ta-da list of all the things you accomplished today. Productivity can be very important to happiness. Whether that means being on top of the laundry or closing a huge deal, you want to feel as though you are in an atmosphere of growth, to see that you're making progress, learning, teaching. A ta-da list helps you feel more cognizant of and satisfied with your day. (You may feel like you did nothing but hey, look! you did do some things!) Ta-da lists are also a great exercise at the end of the year, if you have the discipline. (Whip out your calendar to help with this one.) There might have been days or even weeks when you felt unproductive, but when you look back at a whole year it's staggering to see how much you *did* do.

··· **13** ···

UP YOUR INTERPERSONAL GAME

REMEMBER SOMEONE'S NAME

"One of the most important business etiquette and networking skills, maybe just a human being skill, is the ability to confidently remember someone's name."

—Jim Kwik

1. *Believe* that you can remember names. The only way we can change behaviors or achieve tasks is if we believe we can, because a belief is a signal to your brain to perform a task.
2. *Exercise.* It takes 30–60 days to master a new habit, so practice remembering the names of those you meet as often as you can.
3. *Say it.* As soon as someone introduces themselves, repeat their name back to them—"Hello, Ted."
4. *Use it.* Try to use their name in the conversation 3–4 times. The catch: It has to be done organically or you'll sound super weird.
5. *Ask* if it's a unique name. Ask how they got it. (Is it a family name? Does it mean something special to their parents?) This can help jog your memory the next time you meet. And people *love* talking about themselves.
6. *Visualize.* Most people are better at remembering faces than they are names. The trick is to pair the face you remember with

a visual that cues their name. If someone is named Mary, you could picture her carrying two little lambs, cuing the nursery rhyme and hopefully her name in your next encounter.

7. *End.* Make sure you end the first encounter or conversation using their name: "See ya, Mary, nice to meet you!"

THE EXPERT:

Jim Kwik is a memory and speed reading expert, an international speaker, and the CEO of Kwik Learning, a consulting firm that teaches memory training to help people and businesses achieve more in less time. He is the author of *Limitless: Upgrade Your Brain, Learn Anything Faster, and Unlock Your Exceptional Life.*

THE EXPLANATION:

The steps (believe, exercise, say it, use it, ask, visualize, end) spell out BE SUAVE, which is exactly what you are when you remember people's names. Remembering names is a skill—it takes effort. The good news is it doesn't take as much as you think. The reason you say a person's name is so you hear it twice right up front. This also ensures that you didn't mishear or misunderstand. You don't want to have a twenty-minute conversation with Ted and say, "Good-bye, Ed"—it's better to get corrected right away. And use it in the conversation as much as it makes sense contextually. (Bonus if someone walks by and you can introduce them.) Saying it again when you leave is key as it's one more opportunity for you to use it—and therefore remember it next time—and it will leave Ted with a great impression of you.

Pro tip: Don't tell yourself you're bad at remembering people's names. Your brain is like a supercomputer, and your self-talk is like a program it will run. If you tell yourself you're not good at remembering names, you won't remember the name of the next person you meet because you told your supercomputer not to. A very simple tweak to eliminate negative self-talk is to add the word *yet* at the end: "I'm not good at remembering names *yet*."

WRITE A THANK-YOU NOTE

1. Open with a greeting: "Hi!" "Dear..." "Hey lady!"
2. Immediately state your thanks for the gift or gesture.
3. Add something specific about the gift—how you'll use it or what you love most about it.
4. Look ahead to the future—mention the next time you'll see the person, or that you hope they have a great holiday: "Can't wait to see you at Susie's wedding!"
5. Restate your appreciation: "Thanks again for your thoughtfulness."
6. End with your regards. "XOXO." "Love..." "Peace out."
7. Add a P.S. if that's your thing, something short that makes the person feel good, an inside joke or a nod to what's going on in their life: "P.S., love the bangs."

THE EXPERT:

Cheree Berry is the CEO and creative director of Cheree Berry Paper. She designs gorgeous and highly personalized wedding invitations, holiday cards, baby announcements, and pretty much anything else you might put on paper—even lunchbox notes for kids!

THE EXPLANATION:

When people open a note, they want to know what it's for, so get right to the point (after all, it may have been a while since they gave the gift). Then say something specific about it. When a note says, "Thank you so much for the gift; I can't wait to use it," you're like, "Um, do you even know what I got you? Do you even know who I am?" Details make the recipient feel good. Unless someone got you a Rolex and you really need to gush, simply restate your appreciation at the end and move on to the closing. Add a "P.S." if you're feeling it—they're relevant for almost all correspondence, even most job interviews ("P.S., hope the big pitch meeting was a success."). Don't psych yourself out by over-thinking your message: The whole thing should take about three minutes. If you think of thank-you note writing as something that requires giant blocks of time, it will become a huge chore (and sit on your to-do list for months...or so I've been told). Keep a few cards in your bag and dash one off while you're waiting at the dentist. Oh, and if you're worried about messing up—or using the word *excited* twice—do a rough draft on a device with spell check.

Bonus

Oh, wait, you really *don't* remember what they got you? Avoid a nondescript reference to the "gift." Instead, shift the focus to the giver, recognizing his or her thoughtfulness in a simple, sin-cere opening. Continue by mentioning something specific about that person, maybe a memory of a previous encounter or conver-sation you had. "Thank you so much for the gift, you thoughtful woman! Your generosity knows no bounds. By the way, loved see-ing your crew at the park last week. Hope Nico and Anya are hav-ing a great summer!" Personalizing a moment you shared conveys your genuineness while also distracting from the absence of the gift details. Cheree's Golden Rule for penning a thank-you: Write to others as you would have them write to you.

KNOW WHAT'S GOING ON IN SPORTS

"You don't have to be fake or lie about your interest, but if you want to participate in something that really brings people together—and one of the last things people care about watching *live*—it's important to have these resources."

—Sarah Spain

1. Find a couple sports websites (one for general sports news and one that follows the sports in your particular city) and bookmark them. Check them daily, weekly, or whenever you've got a game or watch party to attend.
2. For schedules, standings, and straightforward information you can rely on and understand, look for trusted news-providing sources that have journalistic standards.
3. If you or your friends are fans of a particular team, flag that team's website/blog/social media page.
4. Follow a few standout athletes on social media.
5. Before a big event, figure out the biggest story lines and read up on those (who's injured, who are the best players, etc). Team-specific websites and blogs are good for this.
6. Always know what's at stake for any particular sporting event—even a Tuesday night baseball game in the middle of May. Why does this game matter? What happens when someone wins or loses? What's the notable history between the teams? What player is currently on the verge of something great?
7. Find the good backstories. Think about what makes the Olympics so fun to watch—you become invested in the athletes after all those lead-up interviews with their families and friends and fifth-grade curling coach.

THE EXPERT:

Sarah Spain is an Emmy- and Peabody Award–winning radio host, TV personality and writer. She's the host of *Spain and Company*, which airs weeknights on national ESPN radio, the host of ESPN's *That's What She Said* podcast, and a *SportsCenter* reporter.

THE EXPLANATION:

Sports brings people together. (It's the very reason all of them were canceled during the coronavirus pandemic!) And if everyone is getting together to watch the NBA finals or the Kentucky Derby, or even…NASCAR, it will be 100 percent more enjoyable and interesting for you if you know what you're watching (the rules, the major players, the rivalries). There are plenty of websites that will give you the snapshots—what's going on today and why you should care—but if you're not used to watching this particular sport (um, NASCAR), the thing that matters at any turn is the stakes. So when in doubt, focus on that. Take the five minutes to understand what the matchup means. Following your team on social media is important because they're going to be posting what games are coming up and retweeting player content—feeling connected to the athletes themselves is a great way to get more invested. And backstories just make everything more engaging. Is this the first time someone is coming back to play where he used to play? Will the whole crowd give him a standing ovation because they love him, even though he's on the other team now? Instead of being like "Wait, what's going on?" you can be part of a cool moment. A little knowledge makes everything more interesting and gives you a reason to care about what you're watching.

COMMENT ON SOCIAL MEDIA

1. Before you comment on anything, ask yourself a simple question: "Would I say this in real life?"
2. Do not derail a conversation. If someone posts about their sick kid or cat don't say, "Yeah, but did you see what's happening to the turtles?" Awful, yes, but not the point.
3. If it's a controversial topic (safe to assume it is), do your homework before chiming in. If you aren't up-to-date on both sides of an issue, perhaps don't chime in at all.
4. Don't try to change someone's mind online. People very rarely back down from an opinion they posted in a comment (i.e., they will die on the sword even if that sword is batshit crazy).
5. For the love of God, check your spelling and grammar. To AVOID THE MOST COMMON GRAMMAR MISTAKES SEE PAGE 209.
6. Use punctuation! Remember that punctuation goes a long way to convey tone. (You know when someone comments "fun" on your vacation photo versus "fun!!!!"? Jerk.)
7. Know that emojis cover a multitude of sins—not only are they acceptable these days, they're almost expected (and necessary—see step 6).
8. Reread what you've written before you post. Consider what you put on the internet as being forever—are you OK with that comment outliving you?
9. Comment on the posts of people who comment on your stuff.

THE EXPERT:

Sara Buckley is the director of social media for the Buzz Brand, a creative agency that helps small businesses expand their social media presence. She also runs the wildly popular Instagram accounts @nottheworstmom and @nottheworstmarriage.

THE EXPLANATION:

The same etiquette you'd use in person should apply online—you wouldn't go to a dinner party and derail the conversation, right? Or chime in on something you have no knowledge of? You'd probably only speak up if it added value to a topic or if you had something interesting (or supportive) to say. Do that online, too. Something to remember about social media: It's forever. And you don't know who's following you—it could be a future employee, a future colleague, a future boss. It's now very normal for prospective employers to look at your social media before or after a job interview. The person you are on the internet is how you're viewed—for better or often worse. So be mindful about what you're posting and commenting on. It can cost you a job; it can cost you a relationship. You have to take this stuff seriously because other people do.

Bonus

Want to grow your brand/business on social? If you're trying to get your name out there and attract more followers, introduce yourself with likes and comments and engagement with other people. Imagine being at a cocktail party when you're just starting out in your industry, and you find out there are other well-established people from your industry at the cocktail party, too. You would introduce yourself and if they talked to you, you would respond. It's the same online. Consider it just another venue for human interaction. This is where your future fans and future followers and future customers are hanging out. You have a free platform to reach people who will buy your stuff, go to your store, download your music (order your book?). Utilize that! But don't just give a thumbs-up—add something to the conversation. If you want people to notice you, be a positive, noticeable presence. (People read the comments—and if they like what they read, they go follow you.)

ARGUE PRODUCTIVELY WITH YOUR PARTNER

1. Ask yourself two questions: "Am I tired? Am I hungry?" Never argue before you can say no to those two things.
2. Decide what you want to resolve and tell your partner the plan.
3. Give yourself a time limit—set an alarm if you have to—and share it. "Let's talk about this for only ten minutes, OK?"
4. Make your point without insults or name-calling. SEE PAGE 46 FOR HOW TO MAKE YOUR POINT HEARD and PAGE 48 FOR HOW TO GIVE CONSTRUCTIVE CRITICISM.
5. Listen without interrupting (i.e., take turns speaking—it feels like an obvious step but, well, relationships).
6. Stick to the subject matter decided in step 2, no matter how much you want to bring up the dishwasher thing again.
7. Come up with an action item that will fix the problem.
8. Set a time line for revisiting the issue.
9. End on a positive note—even if it's forced.

THE EXPERT:

Jo Piazza is a bestselling author, award-winning journalist, and podcast host. Her book *How to Be Married* chronicles various models of marriage across six different continents. Her *Committed* podcast, which has been adapted for television, further dissects marriage and relationships through the stories of inspiring couples who've stuck together despite great odds.

THE EXPLANATION:

Before you begin any conversation or argument make sure you're well-fed and well-rested. No one can function at their best or make rational decisions when they're hungry or tired. Just ask any two-year-old. As Jo aptly puts it, "the old adage 'Don't go to bed angry' is bullshit." You need to set yourself up for success. And make every argument about *one thing*, so you should know what that one thing is going in. That means you resist the urge to data-dump all the past grievances you could easily dig up (so easily!) and have a "safe word" for when you inevitably get off track—think of something funny and meaningful to the two of you that will give you a brief moment of levity. The most important thing to know about arguing is that the listening is the most important part. Give your partner the space to make a point before you start with your counterpoint. And don't end an argument without some kind of resolution or action item. Try to find something that will fix the problem you came in trying to solve. Say, "Hey, let's try what we suggested, see how that works, and revisit this a week or a month from now." Then go have makeup sex. Oh, wait—that's only in the movies.

SAY YOU'RE SORRY

"Apologizing is a critically important life skill; it does so much for the apologizer, too. You're not just saying 'I'm sorry' to appease the other person, you're accepting and owning *your* behavior, which goes a long way toward your own mental well-being."

—Zelana Montminy

1. Think about what, specifically, you did to contribute to the issue (you need to get really clear on the apology you're going to give).
2. Ask the other person to talk at a time when neither of you is busy or distracted. Apologies are best in person, followed by over the phone, with text or email apologies coming in a distant third.
3. Say "I'm sorry for _____." (Fill in the blank with a sincere acknowledgment of what you did wrong—see step 1 if you're unclear.)

4. Resist the urge to make an excuse for your wrongdoing.
5. Mention how things will be different next time or how you'll attempt to change (again, be specific).
6. Ask, "Can you forgive me?"
7. Ask how they think you can best move forward—what does the other person need from you?

THE EXPERT:

Zelana Montminy, Psy.D., is a behavioral scientist and positive psychologist. She's the author of *21 Days to Resilience*, is on the advisory board of Common Sense Media and is a go-to authority in the media world with speaking engagements at universities, corporations, and nonprofits worldwide.

THE EXPLANATION:

Apologizing is about fixing a wrong, and saying sorry is just the beginning. But it's a hugely important step, which is why taking time to hone your message is so critical. Realizing exactly how you hurt that person is important. Sometimes, if the issue is with your partner, that may mean going to bed angry and revisiting the issue—and the apology—the next day with a clearer head. You have to talk to people at the right time; otherwise, the apology will fall flat. And don't say, "I'm sorry *you* feel this way" or "It's because *you* did X." In fact, avoid *you* statements altogether and focus on *I* statements. Then hear them out, and don't interrupt to defend yourself. This is not a time to blame or make any excuses whatsoever ("Oh, it's because you did this and that's why I did that" or "I'm so stressed out at work and I just can't deal and that's why I did that shitty thing to you"). An apology is pretty meaningless if nothing changes afterward, so brainstorm with this person on how you can avoid the problem in the future. Be prepared to do what it takes if the relationship is important to you.

GET OUT OF A CONVERSATION YOU DON'T WANT TO BE IN

1. Signal that you're stepping away by extending your hand for a shake or, better yet, a pat on the shoulder or a little wave.

2. Say, "Great to chat but I've gotta run." (You can ask for their business card, tell them you'll follow up—if you will—or say you can talk more later or at X date, if you want to.)

3. Simply walk away.

4. If it's gossipy or political, you can be honest and say, "I'm not comfortable with the direction of this conversation" or "I need to take a break, please excuse me."

5. If you're stuck with a person who's monopolizing the conversation, try: "It was nice talking to you. I want to say hello to a few people, so I will catch up with you later."

6. If it's a party, don't say you're going to go grab something at the buffet or the bar (they might go with you!).

7. If it's a group you need to get away from, you can quickly and quietly interject by waving your hand up to signal and loudly whispering, "Hey it's been great talking to you all but I've gotta go." Then just leave.

8. Don't apologize. You can say, "Excuse me for interrupting, I'm going to need to run," but you're not doing anything wrong by ending a conversation so a sorry isn't necessary.

9. If you see someone you know in the vicinity you can say, "Oh, I need to run, I have to talk to Kate about something, please excuse me." Then beeline toward Kate.

10. You could also call Kate (or someone else you know who's walking by) over and say, "Oh, there's someone I'd like to introduce you to"—then introduce them and say, "If you'd excuse me, I'm gonna leave you two to chat. I'm going to mix and mingle."

THE EXPERT:

Diane Gottsman is a national etiquette expert and the author of *Modern Etiquette for a Better Life*. She's the founder of the Protocol School of Texas, a company specializing in executive leadership and business etiquette training.

THE EXPLANATION:

Whether it's your mom, a coworker, another parent at the bus stop, or the guy in line at the dry cleaner, closing a conversation has the same general rules: Be direct, polite, and sincere. In some cases, you'll be doing the other person a favor. Extending your hand (or patting them on the shoulder or waving) signals, "I gotta go," and physically puts a barrier between you—it's a body language indicator you're moving on. Everyone must be responsible for their own boundaries, so if you're in a conversation that's uncomfortable (gossip, political rant, argument), say whatever is most comfortable for you to exit the conversation. You don't have to overthink this. "Hey Sarah, I'm going to have to run. I will talk to you tomorrow" is a perfectly polite way to peace out.

Bonus

How to say hello to someone on the train (without having to sit with them): Smile. Wave and say hello. Keep walking. If it's someone you feel necessary to say more to, add: "Great seeing you. I'm on a mission to catch up on a few emails. Talk soon?" It should be as simple as that. Not necessary to sit next to them or carry on a lengthy conversation—and remember, they probably don't want to sit with you any more than you want to sit with them.

How to end a phone call: When it comes to closing out a conversation on the telephone, the other person can't see your body language or facial expressions, so you have to jump in and guide the conversation to a close. Politely interrupt by saying something like "Karen, I'm expecting another call and I need to prepare. I'll follow up with you in the next couple of days to see how the project is moving along." Keep it short and sweet but authentic. And don't say you're going to call back if you don't plan to return a call.

HAVE YOUR WORDS READY WHEN YOU'RE TELLING PEOPLE ABOUT A TRICKY SITUATION

"Searching for the right words over and over can be mentally draining. Instead, have them precooked so you have a crisp message that both relieves the stress of having to talk about it and communicates what *you* want to communicate."

—Gretchen Rubin

1. Identify the thing you know people are going to be asking you about—a breakup, a health issue, an unexpected job change.
2. Decide how to frame the situation. "How do I want to think about it for myself? How do I want to frame it for other people? How do I want this information to go out into the world?"
3. Come up with 2–3 sentences that succinctly sum up the situation. Include the basic facts. Not sure what people will want to know? Ask yourself: What would *you* be curious about if the tables were turned? Write them down if that helps!
4. Offer one sentence on how you *feel* about the situation because that's what people are most interested in. How are you handling this? How are you dealing with it?
5. Pay attention to your tone of voice on your delivery. If you're matter-of-fact, it closes the conversation; injecting humor can invite further questions.
6. Repeat as needed.

THE EXPERT:

Gretchen Rubin is the author of *The Happiness Project*, *Happier at Home*, *Better Than Before*, *The Four Tendencies*, and *Outer Order, Inner Calm*. She's the host of the award-winning podcast *Happier with Gretchen Rubin*, where she shares insights, strategies, and stories to help people understand themselves and create a happier life.

THE EXPLANATION:

Often the anxiety of whatever we're facing makes us want to shut ourselves off and avoid being questioned. It can be exhausting when other people are constantly asking you how you're feeling and what's going on—eventually, if it's something that's hard to think about, it can feel like it takes a lot out of you to even put it into words. Taking the time to craft your message isn't being inauthentic, it's about mindfully deciding how *you* want to characterize the situation. Example: "John and I are getting a divorce. It's not what I would have chosen, but now that it's happening I feel a sense of freedom." Having a statement like this, a complete tiny little package, helps you stay on message for yourself and other people and also makes it easier to *end* a conversation. If you don't want to keep talking about it, there's a definitive quality to it, like a statement from a government office: "We will take no further questions at this time." It shuts it down but in a nice way. Of course, with close friends and family you can talk on and on about how you feel, but this way you're prepared and you don't have to feel assaulted by fresh statements every time.

Bonus

This works for good news, too. Telling people about a new job, an engagement, the super-fun-but-also-life-changing book you're writing, whatever! Preparing your elevator pitch ahead of time enables *you* to control the narrative and be able to present yourself to the world in the way you want to be perceived. It also just makes for smoother small talk when you have your words at the ready.

SUPPORT A FRIEND WHEN THEY TELL YOU SOMETHING CRAPPY THEY'RE DEALING WITH

1. Keep your reaction neutral. If someone is being vulnerable with you, don't respond with shock or disapproval, particularly if what they just told you is private and/or a source of shame (cheating, lying, getting fired, trouble with the law, etc.).
2. Ask: "Do you want to talk about it?"
3. If they do, follow with gentle questions: "So, how are you feeling about it?" or "How has it been for you?"
4. Don't push for all the details—the particulars of exactly how things came about aren't as important as how your friend is *feeling* about what happened.
5. Keep your focus on them and listen; your job is to *hear*, not to respond (meaning as they're talking, don't be thinking about what you're going to say next—this is an essential life skill and it ain't easy).
6. Avoid giving unsolicited advice. People usually just want to vent, not problem-solve, and offering your opinion can imply that you know more about the situation than they do, which won't always be the case. (You can *ask* if they'd like your advice, though—something soft and noncondescending, like "Would it be helpful to hear what I might do in your position?" or "Do you want my thoughts or do you just want to vent?")
7. When in doubt, say, "I'm really sorry this happened/you're dealing with this right now." People are afraid of saying "I'm sorry" because they think it's cliché, but if you're genuine and authentic that sentiment will come through.
8. Finish with "How can I best support you right now?"
9. Check in on them tomorrow. And the next day. And the day after that.

THE EXPERT:

Rachel Wilkerson Miller is the author of *The Art of Showing Up: How to Be There for Yourself and Your People* and *Dot Journaling: A Practical Guide*. A former BuzzFeed senior editor, she's now a deputy editor at Vice.

THE EXPLANATION:

First things first: Withhold judgment and fight the urge to drop your jaw or say "Whaaaaaa??!!" Don't make assumptions about how they're feeling about this news either way. (They may be *thrilled* about their divorce, and if you look all Debbie Downer they could feel bad for not being more devastated.) You could say "Wow, that's big news," which totally gets you out of having the wrong emotional reaction and it lets the person tell you where they are. Asking gentle questions is a good way to start because it will help you figure out what they need from you at that moment. And focus on their feelings, not the facts. This idea comes from the book *There Is No Good Card for This* by Kelsey Crowe and Emily McDowell (EMILY IS ON PAGE 214 OF THIS BOOK!). You don't want to get in the weeds of a medical diagnosis or their next job application process because that's not really the point right now. Yes, some friends *will* hash out the whole thing at length, so be prepared for that, too—but just let them talk. And never feel bad asking them what they need from you if it's not clear. Sometimes it's advice, sometimes it's just to listen, sometimes they need a distraction, or maybe it's something really practical like, say, a ride to court.

Bonus

Send a puzzle. When it feels like the world is falling apart, literally putting something back together can be powerful. Why do you think so many of us were doing puzzles in quarantine? Puzzles are equal parts soothing and stimulating. They're also a challenge, but it always feels like a friendly one. They are an incredibly pure way to begin healing a broken heart and to occupy a mind that would otherwise be consumed by thoughts of loss, anger, fear, or simply the notifications on your phone. A puzzle won't solve all of your problems, but a puzzle is a problem you can solve.

OFFER CONDOLENCES

"Know that you can't say anything that will fix this, so take the pressure off yourself; your goal isn't to find the most comforting words possible, it's simply to acknowledge this person's pain."
—Nora McInerny

1. Just do it. Now. (The worst thing you can say is nothing.)
2. Send a text or mail a card or pick up the phone or, better yet, show up.
3. Simply state the facts: "This is awful. My heart hurts for you. I'm here if you want to talk. And if you don't." (A simple "I'm so sorry to hear about X" works, too—use the person's name or "your mom/your friend/your uncle" instead of the general "your loss.") Don't rush to change the subject or make a joke. Let the silence sit there. This may be uncomfortable for you, but the mood is not yours to lighten; let the griever grieve.
4. Share a nice memory or anecdote about the person who died if you knew them.
5. If you're close and want to do something else, make sure it feels authentic (i.e., if you've never changed a diaper in your life, don't offer to watch the baby).
6. Put this date in your calendar and reach out again next year.

THE EXPERT:

Nora McInerny is the host of the podcast *Terrible, Thanks for Asking* and author of *No Happy Endings* and *It's Okay To Laugh (Crying Is Cool Too)*. When she was thirty-one, Nora miscarried her second baby and lost her dad to cancer, and then her husband, Aaron, died from a brain tumor, all within weeks of each other. Her TED Talk on grief saw over 2.5 million views in its first year. She's the cofounder of the Hot Young Widows Club, for people who lost their significant other.

THE EXPLANATION:

There's a hierarchy to condolences. At the very lowest level, you can dash off a text or an email or a DM. At the midrange you can send a handwritten card.[4] And the highest level of care and participation is that you SHOW UP. You go to the funeral. You sit shiva. You bring a hot dish and you offer a hug. When actually talking, remember this: They don't need to be told a story about your own life and your own loss. They don't need to be told what their loss means—that's for them to define. And they don't need to be told how to fix it (don't *should* on them). Even if you say something truly abhorrent like "Everything happens for a reason" or "It's God's plan," it's a sign you tried. You showed up. And just being there is *huge*. (P.S. No one really knows what to say, not you and not the person experiencing the grief—so an "I don't really know what to say; I just know I want to be here for you" is totally acceptable.) If you can share something nice about their person, great. But don't

---

4. Just always send a card. Even if you didn't know the person who died. Even if it's to a coworker you think hates you. "I heard about XYZ. I want you to know I'm thinking about you." You don't need to describe how awful it is—they know how it feels. You don't have to add a religious platitude—unless you're inclined and know one will be appreciated. You don't have to write much else. Address it, stamp it, send it.

just share it at the funeral when people are zonked out and unable to take in new information; mention it months, even years, later. Don't be afraid to say a dead person's name and talk about their life, not just their death. One of the things people are most afraid of when they lose someone is that they're going to lose *more* of them, so sharing your memories helps keep them alive.

Bonus

Don't say or write, "Let me know if you need anything." A person who's deeply in grief doesn't know what they need. If you really want to do something more, just do it. But this requires some mental math: Who are you to this person? What are your skills? What can you reliably and realistically follow up on? Do that. Even if it's just showing up to shovel their walkway in the winter, or sending gift cards in the mail. Maybe it's adding their kids to your carpool. Whatever you can do and is naturally an extension of your relationship, do that. And not everything has to be a specifically grief-related offering. You can treat this person like they're still a person, which they are. (When Nora's husband, Aaron, died someone sent her a spa gift certificate and at first she was like, huh...but then she used it a month later for a massage, and it was just what she didn't know she needed.) And if you donate, or drop something off, or send a text or a gift and you don't get a thank-you back, you cannot take that personally.

Pro tips:

- If you run into someone and they tell you about the death or they call to tell you, but you already know, don't say, "I know." You may think that's helping them, but it's actually not allowing them to tell you more, to tell you *their* experience. Instead, say, "I heard but I haven't heard it from *you*." And then let them tell you more if they want to.

- There's no statute of limitations on offering condolences. If you haven't seen this person in months or years, even, but you know their mom died, you should still acknowledge that loss. It's so easy to avoid, and you might think you don't want to ruin their day by bringing it up, but you're missing out on a human connection that can be so wonderful.

- Grief is a chronic condition, so continue to check in. The average American with a full-time job with benefits gets three to five business days after the death of a spouse or a child or a parent. They're back at work and they look normal, so they've gotta be fine, right? They are not fine.

··· 14 ···

FINISH THE DAY STRONG

UNPLUG FROM YOUR PHONE

"Given how profound an impact our relationship to technology has on our well-being, Thrive Global has a lot of Microsteps—too-small-to-fail changes you can immediately incorporate into your daily life—for unplugging. My favorite is to charge your phone outside your bedroom at night."

—Arianna Huffington

1. In addition to making sure you're unplugged at night by escorting your devices outside your bedroom before bed, it's also great to start your day unplugged. And it's easy—when you wake up, instead of looking at your phone right away, take just a minute or two to breathe deeply or set your intentions for the day. Book-ending your day like this will affect all the time in between.

2. Turn off all notifications, except from those who need to reach you. The more our phones buzz at us, the more they condition us to release cortisol, the stress hormone.

3. Do an audit of your phone's home screen to reduce distractions. Take just a few minutes to determine which apps you really need to access. Keep only tools that add value—not apps designed to consume more of your attention.

4. Put away your phone and look up while commuting or running errands. Unplugging while on the move will help you connect with people, sights, and scenes around you—and take stock of what you're grateful for.

5. Take a daily "tech time out" to improve your focus and reduce your stress. Set aside time to step away from your social media and your email so you can truly focus on what you are working on or truly connect with yourself and your loved ones.

6. Schedule time on your calendar for something that matters to you—outside of work. Whether it's going to the gym, going to an art gallery, or seeing family or friends, setting a reminder will help you hold yourself accountable.

7. Mealtimes are also an important time to unplug. One Microstep to try: If you're eating out with friends, play the "phone stacking game." Put your phones in the middle of the table. Whoever looks first picks up the check! But really, anytime you're with someone else—children, family, friends, even colleagues in a meeting—is a time to unplug. You'll be more present and make the most of your time.

THE EXPERT:

Arianna Huffington, founder and CEO of Thrive Global, the founder of *The Huffington Post*, and the author of fifteen books, including, most recently, *Thrive* and *The Sleep Revolution*. In 2016, she launched Thrive Global, a leading behavior-change tech company with the mission of changing the way we work and live by ending the collective delusion that burnout is the price we must pay for success.

THE EXPLANATION:

"There's no set amount of times you should unplug—the important thing is that you build time to unplug and recharge into your day and schedule. Recharging ourselves by unplugging should be as routine and habitual as it is for us to recharge our phones by plugging them. Unplugging is important because disconnecting from the world—or at least the digital, screen-bounded version of it—is the only way we can truly connect with others and, especially, ourselves. Unplugging allows us to tap into our natural creativity and wisdom. It allows us to find the calm center of strength in the middle of the storm. And it's also a key element to lowering stress and avoiding burnout, which is a global epidemic in our modern world."—Arianna Huffington

FORGIVE SOMEONE AND LET GO

"We let people into our heads that we would never let into our homes, and they can do a lot of damage in there. We need to stop inviting them in."

—davidji

1. Recognize the unhealthy thought patterns that are taking over your consciousness (you know the ones).
2. Acknowledge the toxic thoughts and feelings bubbling up toward this person, but resist the urge to spew that anger back in their direction. Revenge will not help.
3. Realize that your reaction is a *choice*, and you're choosing to let this person into your thoughts and to cast a dark cloud on your everyday life.
4. Understand that other people's hurtful words or actions stem from their own thoughts and reality; it has nothing to do with you, so you don't have to take it personally.
5. Every time their words come into your awareness, because they still will, smile and say, out loud if you need to, "Oh, hello, visiting again? I think I'll let you go right out the back door." Repeat as many times as needed.

6. At night, before bed, say out loud, "I release _____ from my thoughts."

7. In the morning, when you wake up, repeat it. (You're giving yourself permission to free yourself from the hold you've allowed this person to have on you.)

8. Continue to train your brain to release these thoughts and know that on the other side of forgiveness is *freedom*—your thoughts will be yours to direct toward the positive things and people in life.

THE EXPERT:

davidji is an internationally recognized stress-management expert, meditation teacher, and author of *destressifying: The Real-World Guide to Personal Empowerment, Lasting Fulfillment, and Peace of Mind.*

THE EXPLANATION:

Holding on to a grudge is like drinking poison and expecting someone else to die. You have 60,000 to 80,000 thoughts a day; if 30,000 of them are about this person, it's time to let go. Forgiveness has very little to do with the other person—it comes from within. And when we forgive, we free ourselves from the ties that connect us to the pain that person caused us. If you're holding on so tightly to that thread, you're losing sight of other, more important things in your life (i.e., the people in your front row). You may say, "I'm not inviting the thoughts in; they just keep pushing their way in and attacking." Forgiveness is a practice and something you have to actively choose to do, over and over, until it takes. There may be a particular person or a particular issue that really requires work— stick with it.

Bonus

Forgiving and moving on doesn't mean you condone the behavior of someone who's hurt you. But it does allow you to release yourself from that hurt. Someone else may have been responsible for creating the moment, but we are the ones left holding on to those words or actions. So we are the ones who have to let it go. Give yourself permission to loosen your grip on the hold they have on you by giving them a pass. Say, "I don't think your intention was to actually hurt me, so I'm going to let that go. You happened to have hurt me, or I took it as that; and so, I need to let that go, too." Bottom line says davidji: Your peace is more important than driving yourself crazy trying to understand why something happened the way it did. Let it go.

SET YOURSELF UP FOR A GOOD NIGHT'S SLEEP

1. Set your bedroom alarm clock for one hour *before* your consistent bedtime.
2. When the alarm goes off, go to your bedroom to shut it off.
3. Spend the next 20 minutes taking care of the things that will keep you awake if you don't do them (turning on the dishwasher, locking up, responding to that group chat about drinks).
4. Now take 20 minutes for hygiene—brush, floss, wash, whatever your routine is, do it now. Try to avoid doing this in bright light.
5. Use the last 20 minutes doing some form of relaxation, which could be anything from using a meditation app to prayer to reading a book or watching Bravo.
6. Escort your phone out of your room. SEE PAGE 240 FOR MORE ON UNPLUGGING.
7. Get into bed and get comfortable.
8. Do a "4-7-8" deep breathing exercise—inhale for four seconds, hold your breath for seven seconds, exhale slowly for eight seconds.

9. Repeat step 8 several times.
10. Nighty Night.

THE EXPERT:

Michael J. Breus, Ph.D., aka "the Sleep Doctor" is a renowned sleep expert and author of *The Power of When*.

THE EXPLANATION:

Setting your bedroom alarm clock forces you to go into your room to turn it off, which is a visual and emotional trigger that it's time to get ready for bed. (Did you know you shouldn't use your phone as your alarm clock?) Breaking your nightly wind-down routine into three 20-minute segments creates a predictable pattern that you and your body will come to depend on. If you can't get to everything you want to do for tomorrow in that first twenty minutes, write it down so it's not bouncing around your brain while you're trying to shut down. This list making can become a part of your evening routine to help you feel more organized. Deeply inhaling and holding your breath increases the body's oxygen level, allowing it to work a little less to function. A long, slow exhale has a meditative quality that's inherently relaxing—it's also similar to the pace of breathing your body adopts as you're falling asleep so it nudges your body and mind toward its period of rest.

Bonus

Waking up completely alert at 3 a.m.? One of the main reasons people do this is low blood sugar. If you ate dinner at, say, 7 p.m., 3 a.m. is eight hours since your last meal. That means your body has been fasting the entire time. When your brain thinks you've run out of fuel and your blood sugar drops, it will wake you up by producing the stress hormone cortisol. This helps jump-start the metabolic process, gets you hungry, and wakes you up to eat. One easy solution: Eat a teaspoon of raw honey before bed—it's difficult to metabolize so it helps keep your blood sugar stable longer. (If sugar is not for you, consider guava leaf; it's been shown to help with sleep and blood sugar regulation.)

REVIEW YOUR DAY TO SEE WHAT WORKED... AND WHAT DIDN'T

1. Be still and take a few deep breaths.
2. Walk yourself through the day from the moment you woke up until right now—take mental notes on what you were most grateful for.
3. Reflect on the times in your day when you felt most alive. When were you excited about what you were engaged in? When did you experience a sense of flow?
4. Look back and identify when you felt the most drained. Did something (or someone) frustrate you? When did you feel sluggish?
5. Ask yourself: "When could I have done better today?" (Practice this one with a heavy dose of compassion for yourself.) "Perhaps I could have been kinder to my kids, I could have been more responsive to my coworkers, I could have made it to the gym."
6. Now let *all* of that go. Forgive yourself and others. SEE PAGE 242 ON FORGIVING SOMEONE.
7. Set your intentions for tomorrow. What lessons from today will you take with you to live your day better tomorrow?

THE EXPERT:

Patty Morrissey is the founder of Clear & Cultivate, a therapeutic organizing and lifestyle company based in Huntington, New York.

Patty was dubbed a "Magician" by *CBS This Morning* and "Guru of Tidiness" by the *New York Times*.

THE EXPLANATION:

This daily practice is modeled after the Ignatian spiritual exercise, the Daily Examen. Starting your review with what you're grateful for sets you up to feel fulfilled, abundant, and safe. Feeling all of those things first is important so you can be kind to yourself when looking back on what you could have done better. The idea is to break the day down and focus on the things that enriched your life, and remove or tweak the things that make you feel most drained. This awareness will help you create a space to improve incrementally—it's about taking it *one day at a time* and understanding that sometimes the smallest changes are the most profound. If you're making a commitment to personal growth (if you're reading this book, surprise, you are!), the daily review is a time to check in and see how it's all going. So how's it going?

Acknowledgments

My first and biggest thank-you is to Kristin van Ogtrop, who sent me an out-of-the-blue email at the end of 2018 asking, "Have you ever thought about writing another book?" To which I immediately replied: "Um, YES!" That exchange kicked off the most fun, intense, rewarding two years of my life. Thank you, Kristin, for being such a fabulous agent and for letting me keep more exclamation points than you were probably comfortable with in the proposal. I have loved working with you on this process and can't wait to do it again!!!

Thank you, Leah Miller, whose initial enthusiasm for the book was obvious (and contagious) from our first phone call. I am lucky to have had you championing this book (and me), I loved trading messages about how much we were discovering we really didn't know, and I am eternally grateful that you got my voice (and need for parentheticals). To the lovely Seema Mahanian, whose keen eye and seamless editing guided me when I needed it most: Thank you for being so kind and patient and working with me to shape the book into something I am really proud of.

I'm grateful to the whole team at Grand Central Publishing, especially Jordan Rubinstein, Alana Spendly, Mari Okuda, Xian Lee, Albert Tang, and Haley Weaver, who was such a smart, calming presence at a critical time for the book. I am so proud to be a GCP author.

This book would not be possible without all the incredible experts I interviewed because, well, I am not an expert. For the past year and a half my job was to talk to people about the thing they are most passionate about and to learn how to do that thing better. I am now *very close* to being a fully functioning adult and I owe that to all of you. Thank you all for sharing your wisdom and for not making fun of me when I said things like, "Wait, you put the laundry detergent *where* exactly?"

Lauren Powell was a godsend and helped me transcribe interviews, researched experts, and taught me how to use Google Sheets (and immediately answered my frantic texts and emails when I forgot how to use Google Sheets). And Allison Conte made the proposal look better than I could have imagined.

Thank you to the many friends who helped with my kids, picked up my slack in carpools, sent me encouraging texts, and listened to me talk on and on (and on) about all the cool things I was learning while writing the book. And then checked in to make sure I was still alive when I went dark for too long. Special shout-out to my tribe of girlfriends who were there to read passages, obsess about the cover, and celebrate every tiny milestone of the book writing process with a toast. Cheers, girls!

And thank you to those who went out on a limb for me to put me in touch with some of the incredible experts in the book: Liz Carey, Kara Mendelsohn, Lindsey Weidhorn, Lauren Smith Brody, Suze Yalof Schwartz, Kristin Koch, Kristen Green, Krista DeMaio, Keri Potts, Jennifer Alfson, Gina DeCandia, Jamin Mendelsohn, Margarita Bertsos, Mary Giuliani.

And especially Joanna Parides Sims for going above and beyond to support this book before it was even a book and for pumping me up and believing in me when I was doubting myself. I am so lucky to have you in my corner.

My sisters, Melissa and Meghan, who are always my first readers (even on potential Instragram posts—sorry, girls) and my biggest fans and gave such excellent feedback: Thank you for putting up with me and entertaining my kids and not side texting too much about me during this time. You didn't, right?

My parents, John and Cindy Zammett, and my mother-in-law, Debbie Ruddy, for helping with the kids (and the laundry) and encouraging me, always.

My kids, Alex, Nora, and Molly, who remained quiet during my interviews, didn't fight, cooked their own meals, and never missed the bus while I worked on this book from a makeshift office in our home. Just kidding! But I love you all so much and am really excited to share this book with you. It is required reading and there will be a quiz at the end.

Finally, thank you to my husband, Nick, for holding down the fort and then some because, as it turns out, multitasking while writing is not a life skill I possess. But I can now make a mean cheese board AND fold a fitted sheet, so there's that. I love you and I love our life (even more so now that I have some serious skills to bring to the table).